The Wedding Collection

Low Voice

Compiled and Edited by Richard Walters

On the cover: Georgia O'Keeffe, *Calla*, Oil on board, 1924.
Private collection, southern state, 1998.

ISBN-13: 978-1-4234-1265-6
ISBN-10: 1-4234-1265-6

HAL•LEONARD®
CORPORATION
7777 W. BLUEMOUND RD. P.O. BOX 13819 MILWAUKEE, WI 53213

INDEXED

Visit Hal Leonard Online at
www.halleonard.com

Contents

Pop/Rock Classics

Contemporary Christian

Contents

Alphabetically by Title

INDEXED

Ave Maria

Charles Gounod
adapted from the Prelude in C Major by J.S. Bach

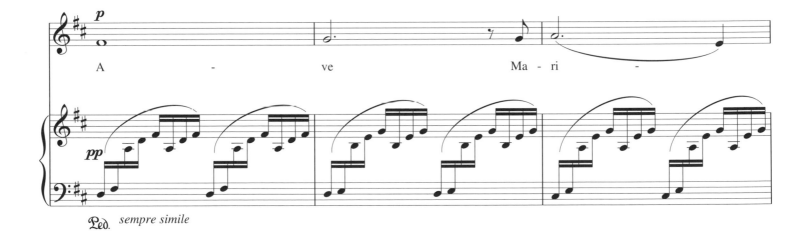

Do - mi - nus te - cum, be - ne -

dic - ta tu in mu - li -

e - ri-bus et _____ bc - ne - dic - tus

fruc - tus _____ ven - tris _____

tu - i Je - sus. _____ Sanc - ta Ma-

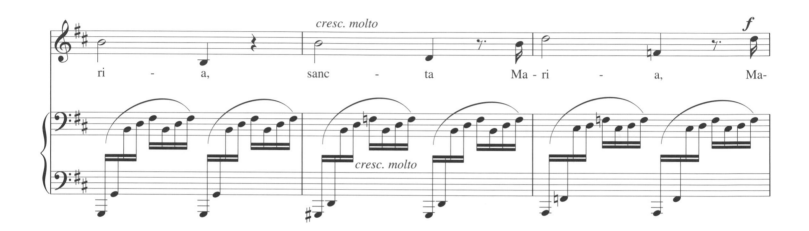

ri - a, sanc - ta Ma - ri - a, Ma-

ri - a, o - ra___ pro no - bis,

no - bis pec - ca - to - ri - bus,

nunc _____ et ___ in ho - ra, in

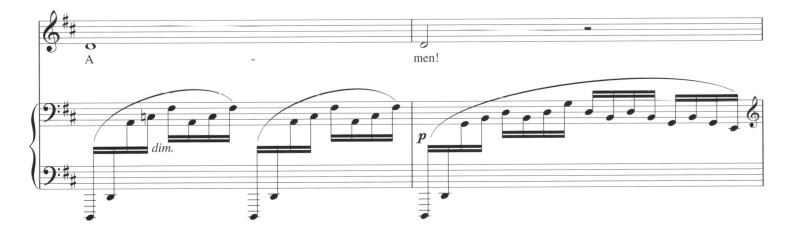

ho - ra _____ mor - tis _____ nos - trae, _____

A - men!

A - men!

Ave Maria

Franz Schubert

* Normally, at a wedding, only sing the first verse.

na, Ma - ri - a__ gra - ti - a
i, O - ra pro __ no - bis pec - ca

ple - na, Ma - ri - a gra - ti - a__ ple -
to - ri - bus, O - ra, o - ra__ pro no -

na, A - ve, _____ A - ve! Do - mi -
bis, O - ra, o - ra__ pro no -

nus, _____ Do - mi - nus__ te - cum, be - ne -
bis _____ pec - ca - to - ri - bus, nunc

dic - ta tu in mu - li - e - ri - bus, et
et in ho - ra _____ mor - tis, in

be - ne - dic - tus, et
ho - ra mor - tis no - strae, in

be - ne - dic - tus fruc - tus ven - tris, ven - tris
ho - ra mor - tis, mor - tis no - strae, in

tu - i, Je - sus.
ho - ra mor - tis no - strae.

A - - - - ve Ma - ri - - -
A - - - - ve Ma - ri - - -

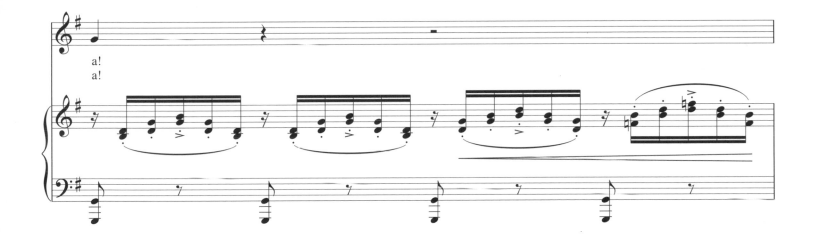

a!
a!

sim.

dim.

Bist du bei mir

(You Are with Me)

Gottfried Heinrich Stölzel
(previously attributed to J.S. Bach)

Anonymous

Bist du ___ bei ___ mir, geh' ich mit
You are ___ with ___ me, my joy for -

Freu - den zum Ster - ben ___ und zu mei - ner ___
ev - er. Un - til ___ my ___ death and un - to my

Ruh', zum _____ Ster - ben und zu mei - ner Ruh'.
rest, un - til ___ death and un - to rest.

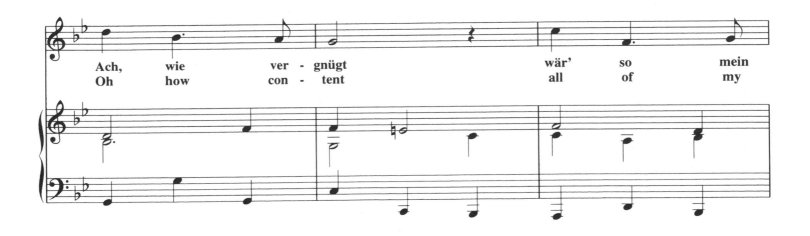

Ach, wie ver - gnügt wär' so mein
Oh wie how con - tent all of my

En - de, Es drück - ten __ dei - ne schö - nen __
earth - ly days, And at __ the __ end will your __ warm and

Hän - de mir __ die ge - treu - en Au - gen zu.
lov - ing hand reach to __ gent - ly __ close my eyes.

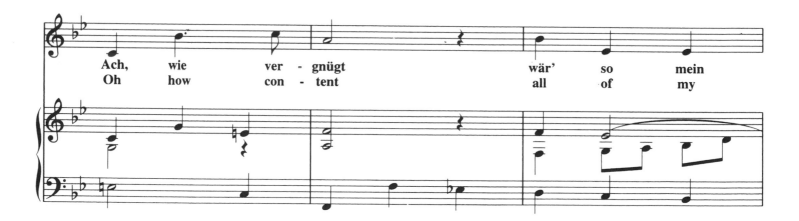

Ach, wie ver - gnügt wär' so mein
Oh how con - tent all of my

En - de, Es drück - ten __ dei - ne schö - nen __
days __ And at __ the __ end will your __ warm and

Hän - de mir _____ die ge-treu - en Au - gen zu.
lov - ing hand reach to _____ gent - ly _____ close my eyes.

Bist du _____ bei _____ mir, geh' ich mit
You are _____ with _____ me, my joy for -

Freu - den, zum Ster - ben _____ und zu mei - ner _____
e - ver. Un - til _____ my _____ death and un - to my

Ruh', zum _____ Ster - ben und zu mei - ner Ruh'.
rest, un - til _____ death and un - to rest.

Dank sei Dir, Herr
(Thanks Be to God)

Siegfried Ochs*
(previously attributed to Handel)

Andante lento, ma non Adagio

Dank _____ sei Dir,
Thanks _____ be to

opt. { Dank _____ } sei Dir, Herr,
{ Herr, Dank _____ }
God, Thanks _____ be to God,

Du hast Dein Volk mit Dir ge - führt, Is -
Thou who has made thy peo - ple free, All

---

*Siegfried Ochs (1858-1929) claimed to have discovered an aria by Handel, and to have made an arrangement of the piece, which was published and became well-known. Closer research has revealed that this is actually an original composition by Ochs.

- ra - el hin durch das Meer.
grate - ful thanks be to Thee.

con espressione

sempre f

Wie ei - ne__ Her - de zog__ es hin - durch,____
Like a__ great_ flock Thy hand__ ev - er led____ us,

Herr,_____ Dei - ne Hand schütz - te es,
Lord,_____ Thy_____ hand hand leads _____ us,

in Dei - ner__ Gü - te_ gabst Du ihm Heil.
By all__ Thy_ good - ness Sal - va - tion is ours.

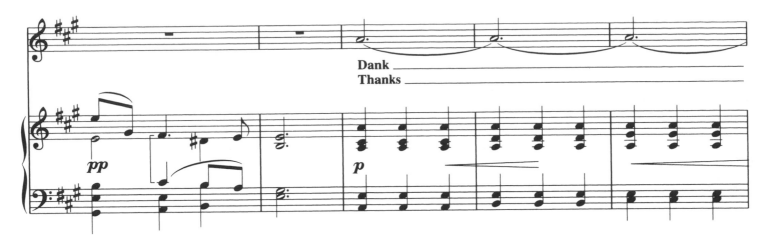

Dank _____
Thanks _____

_ sei Dir, Dank _____ sei Dir,
_ be to God, be to

opt. Herr, Dank _____
Thanks _____

Herr, Du hast Dein Volk mit Dir ge - führt,
God, Thou who has made Thy peo - ple free,

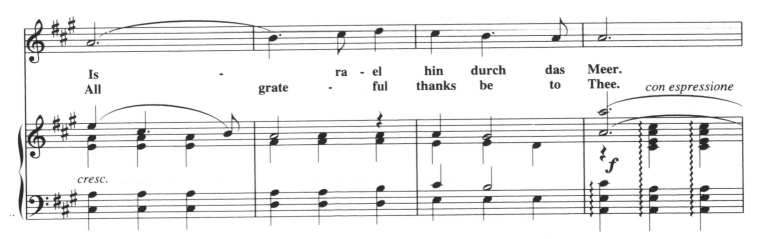

Is - ra - el hin durch das Meer.
All grate - ful thanks be to Thee.

con espressione

Entreat Me Not to Leave Thee
(Song of Ruth)

From the Book of Ruth 1:16-17

Charles Gounod

to re-turn from fol-low-ing af - ter thee, for

whith-er thou go - est I will go, and where thou lodg - est

I will lodge; whith-er thou go - est I___ will go, and

where thou lodg - est ___ I will lodge, where thou lodg - est,

where thou lodg - est, I will lodge. _____ Thy

un poco meno presto, ma pochissimo

peo - ple shall be my peo - ple,

and thy ___ God, my God; _____ thy

peo - ple shall be my peo - ple, and thy

God, _____ my God; _____ Thy

peo - ple shall be my peo - ple, and thy

God, my God. Where thou

di - est, will I die, _____ and there will I be

bur - ied; ___ The Lord do so to me, and more al - so, if aught but

death part thee and me, if aught but death ___ part thee and

me. ___ Thy peo - ple shall be my

peo - ple, and thy ___ God, my

God; _____ Thy peo - ple shall be my

peo - ple, and thy God, _____ my

God; _____ Thy peo - ple shall be my

peo - ple, and thy God, _____ thy

God, my God.

Jesu, Joy of Man's Desiring

J.S. Bach
arranged by John Reed

Because of length, a singer may choose to perform just verse one.

Love ___ most ___ bright,
mu - sic ___ rings!

Drawn by Thee, our souls as - pir - ing
Where the flock, in Thee con - fid - ing,

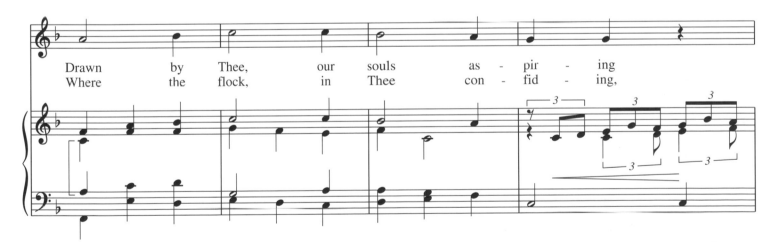

Soar to un - cre - at - ed ___
Drink of joy from death - less ___

light.
springs.

Word   of   God,   our   flesh_____ that   fash - ion'd
Theirs   is   beau - ty's   fair - est   pleas - ure,

With   the   fire   of
Theirs   is   wis - dom's

life _____ im - pas - sion'd.
ho - liest treas - ure.

Striv - ing still to er
Thou dost ev - er

Truth un - known,
lead Thine own,

Soar - ing, dy - ing, round _____ Thy _____
In the love of joys _____ un -

throne.
known.

gratefully dedicated to my friend John Charles Thomas

The Lord's Prayer

Albert Hay Malotte

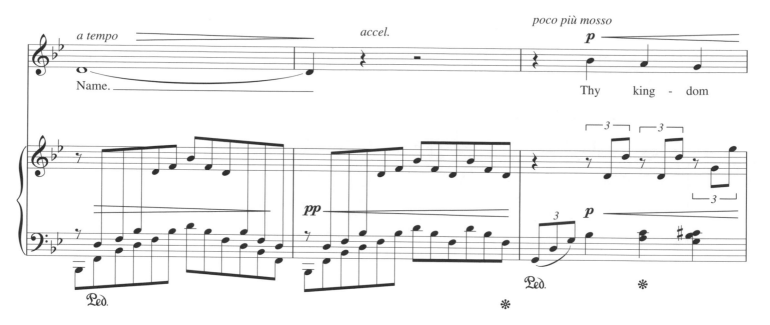

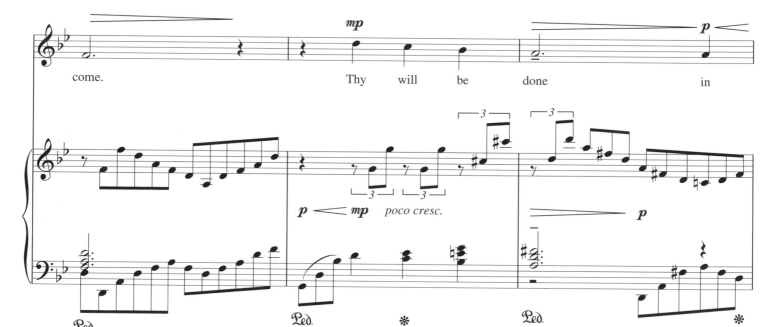

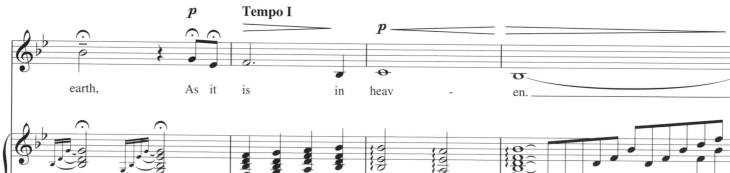

L'istesso tempo

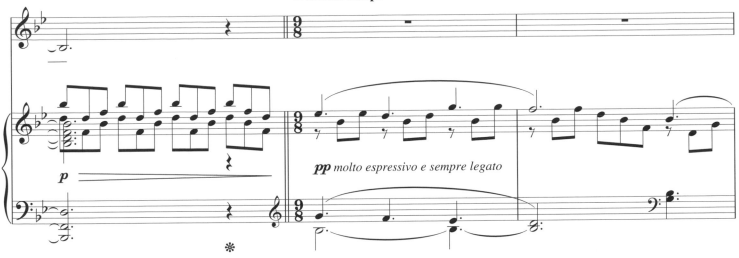

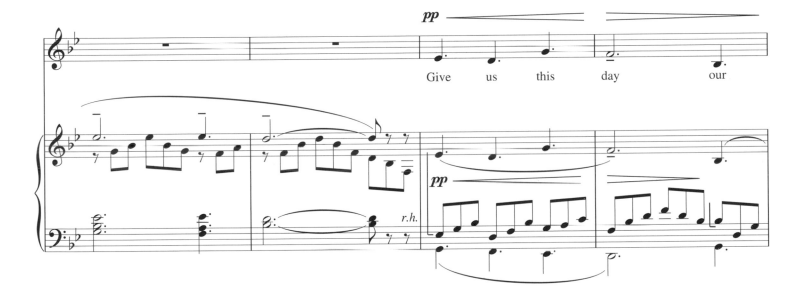

Give us this day our

dai - ly bread. And for-give us our debts, _____ As
tres - pass - es As

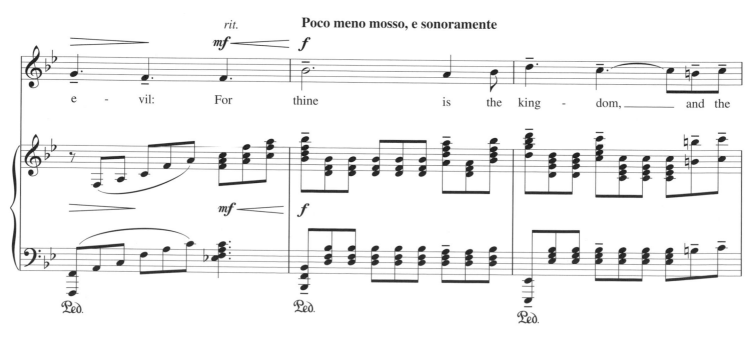

pow - er, _____ and the glo - ry, _____ for

ev - er. _____ A -
and ev - er. A -

Tempo I   *rallentando e morendo*

- men. _____
men. _____

for Gayletha

Now Thank We All Our God

Martin Rinckart, c. 1636
translated by Catherine Winkworth, 1858

"Nun danket alle Gott"
melody by Johann Crüger, 1648
altered by Felix Mendelssohn, 1840
arranged by Richard Walters

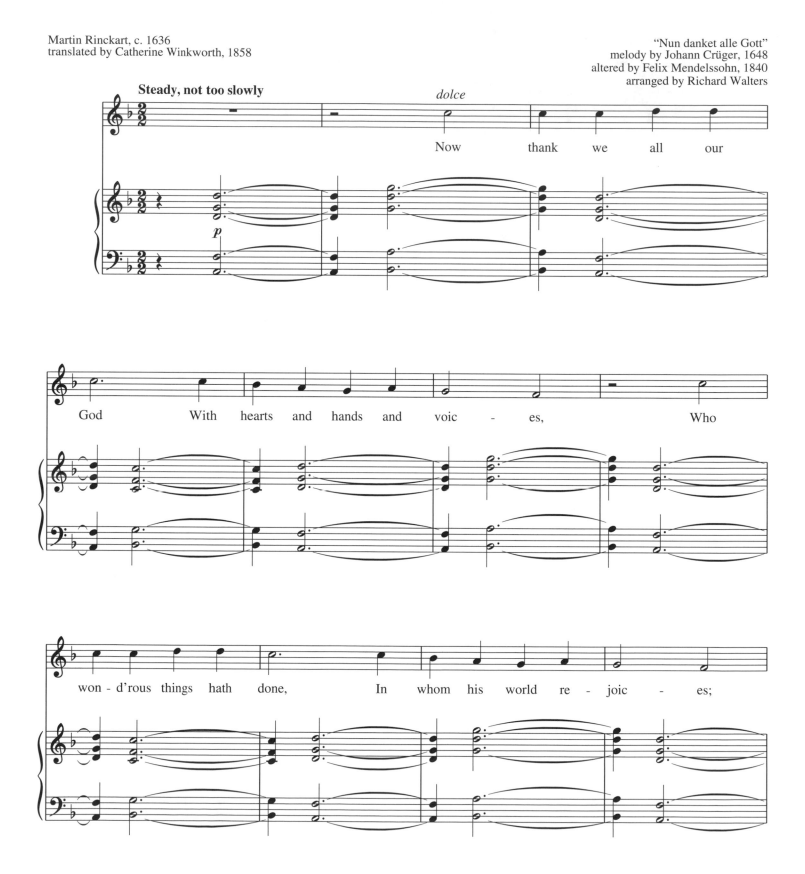

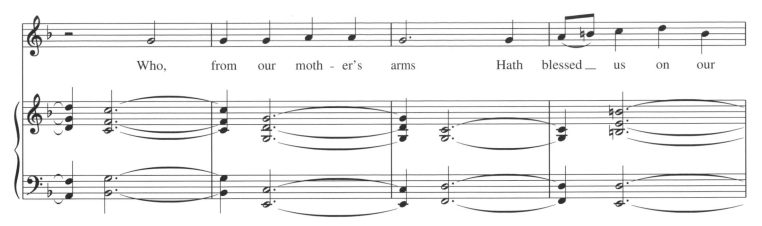

Who, from our moth-er's arms Hath blessed us on our

way With count-less gifts of love, And still is ours to-

poco rit.

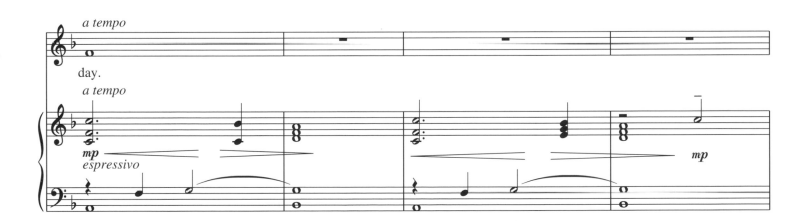

day.

a tempo

mp espressivo

O may this boun-teous God Through all our life be

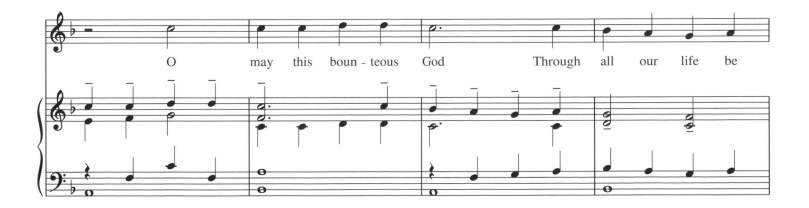

near us, With ev - er joy - ful

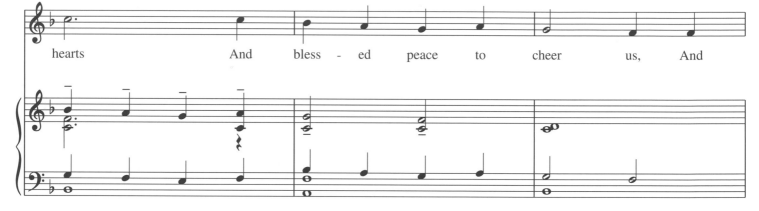

hearts And bless - ed peace to cheer us, And

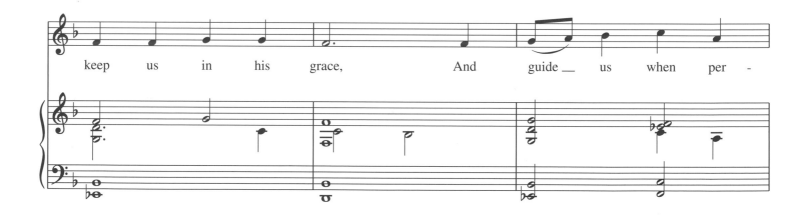

keep us in his grace, And guide __ us when per -

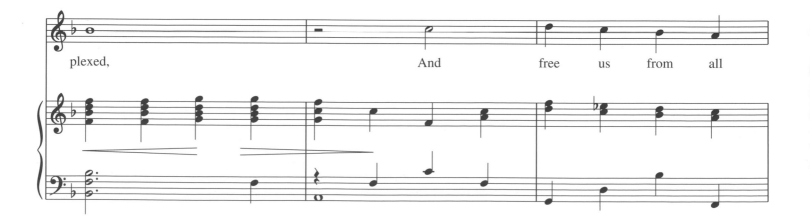

plexed, And free us from all

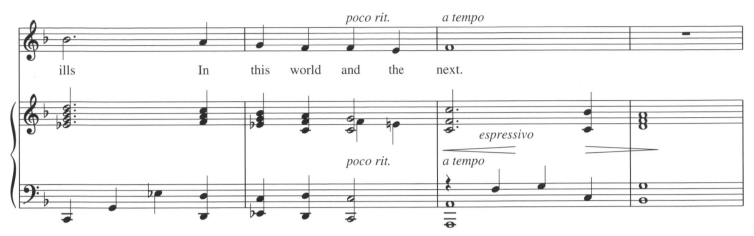

ills   In   this   world   and   the   next.

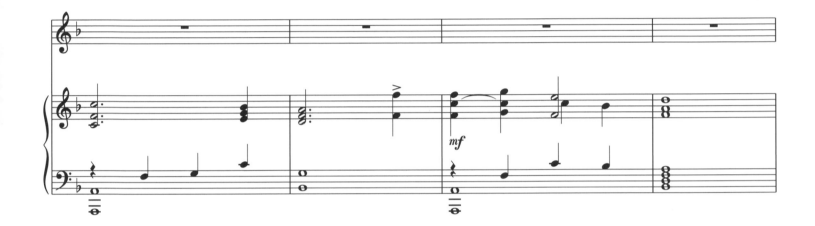

All   praise and thanks to   God   The

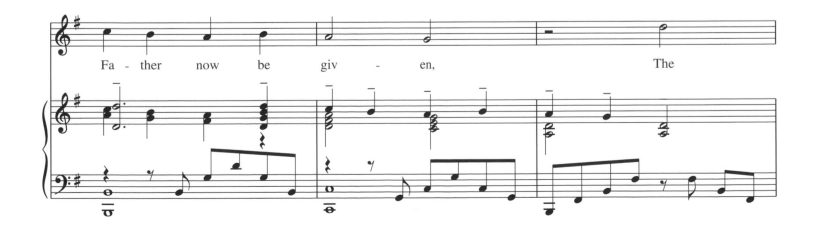

Fa - ther now be giv - en,   The

44

Panis Angelicus

César Franck

ge - li -cus   fit pa - nis ho - mi-num,

Dat pa - nis coe - li-cus fi - gu - ris ter - mi -

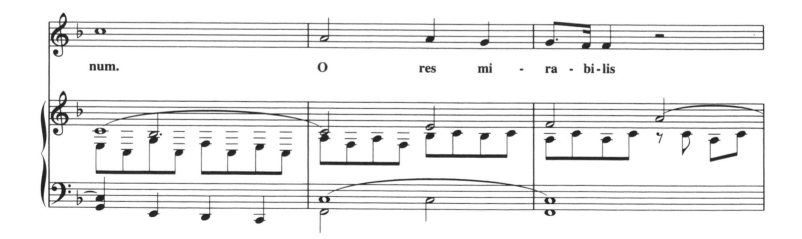

num.   O res mi - ra - bi -lis

man - du - cat Do - mi-num, Pau - per,

pau - per, ser - vus et hu - mi - lis,

Pau - per, pau - per, ser - vus et hu - mi -

lis.

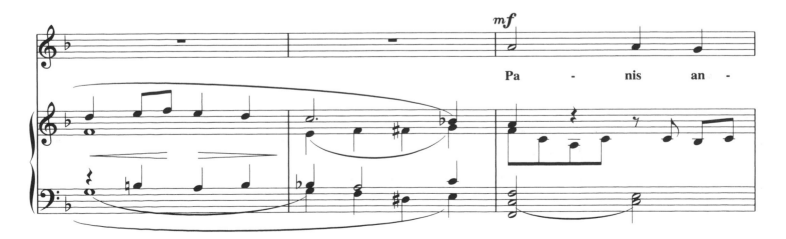

Pa - nis an -

ge - li - cus   fit   pa - nis   ho - mi - num,

Dat   pa - nis   coe - li - cus   fi - gu   ris ter - mi -

num.   O   res   mi - ra bi - lis,

man - du - cat   Do - mi - num   Pau - per, ___

pau - per, ser - vus et hu - mi - lis,

Pau - per, __ pau - per, ser - vus, __ ser - vus et

hu - mi - lis.

Pur ti miro, pur ti godo

from *L'incoronazione di Poppea*

Claudio Monteverdi
realization by Richard Walters

3 **Allegretto**

Io son tua, spe - me mia,
I am yours, all my hope

Tu son io, dil - lo,
I am yours, say to

dil - lo, di', spe - me mia, dil - lo, di',
say to me you are mine, all my hope,

di', tu sei pur, l'i - dol mio, tu sei
me you are mine, my de - sire, you are

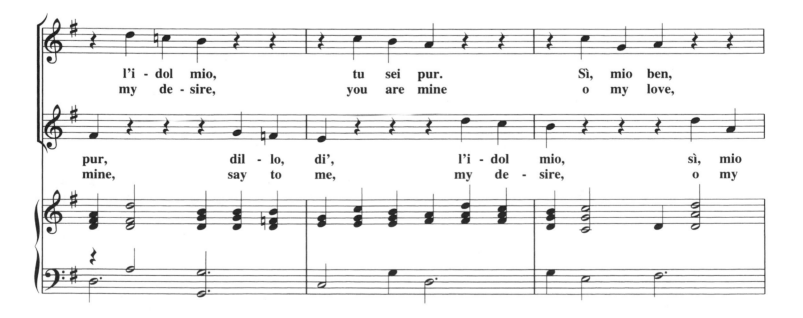

l'i - dol mio, tu sei pur. Sì, mio ben,
my de - sire, you are mine o my love,

pur, dil - lo, di', l'i - dol mio, sì, mio
mine, say to me, my de - sire, o my

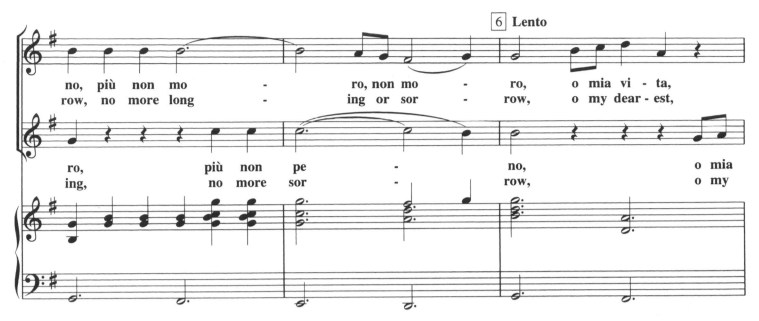

All Good Gifts
from the Musical GODSPELL

Words and Music by
Stephen Schwartz

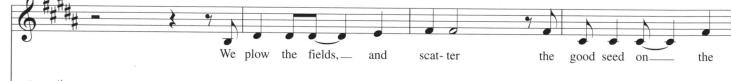

We plow the fields, and scat-ter the good seed on the

land, but it is fed and wa-tered by God's al-might-y hand.

He sends the snow—— in win - ter, the warmth to swell—— the grain, the breez-es and—— the sun - shine, and soft, re - fresh - ing rain.——————— All good gifts a - round—— us—— are sent from

heav - en a - bove.＿＿＿＿＿＿＿＿＿ Then thank the

Lord, O, thank＿ the Lord for all his love.＿＿＿

We thank thee, then O Fa- ther, for all things bright and good, the

seed time and the har - vest, our life, our health, our

food. No gifts have we to of - fer for all thy love im -

parts, but that which thou de - sir - est, our

hum - ble thank - ful hearts.

All good gifts a - round us

are sent from heav - en a - bove.

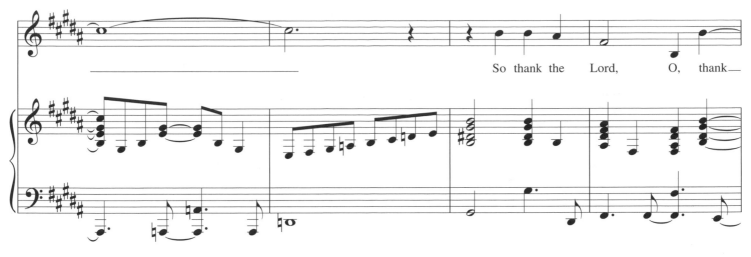

So thank the Lord, O, thank

the Lord for all his love.

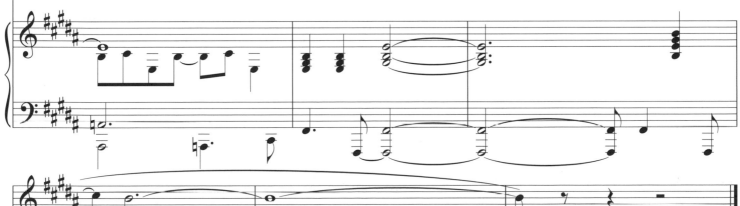

f

I thank you Lord,

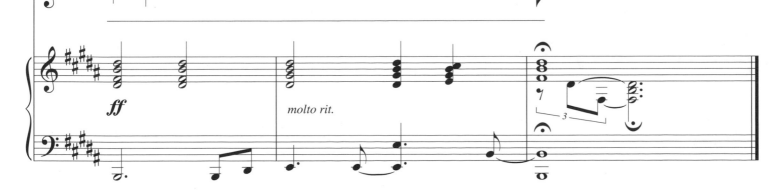

ff *molto rit.*

All I Ask of You
from THE PHANTOM OF THE OPERA

Music by Andrew Lloyd Webber
Lyrics by Charles Hart
Additional Lyrics by Richard Stilgoe

here, with you, be-side you, to guard you and to guide you.

CHRISTINE:

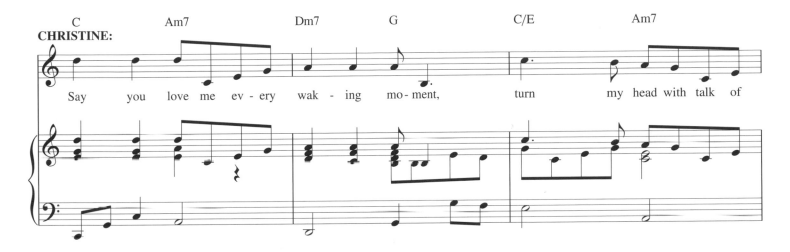

Say you love me ev-ery wak-ing mo-ment, turn my head with talk of

sum-mer-time. Say you need me with you now and al-ways;

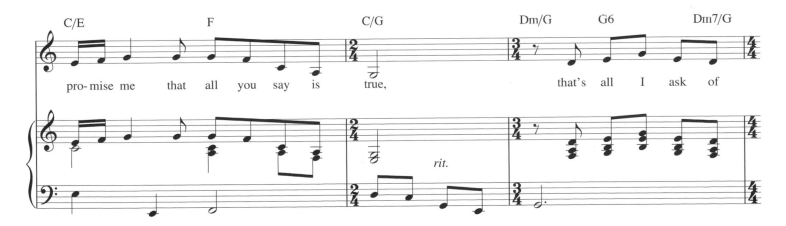

pro-mise me that all you say is true, that's all I ask of

64

RAOUL:
Let me be your shel-ter, let me be your light; you're safe, no one will find you your
you.
a tempo
mf

fears are far be-hind you. All I want is free-dom, a world with no more night; and

CHRISTINE:

you, al-ways be-side me, to hold me and to hide me. Then say you'll share with me one

RAOUL:

love, one life-time; let me lead you from your sol-i-tude.

RAOUL:

do. **CHRISTINE:** Love me, that's all I ask of you.

molto rit. *a tempo*

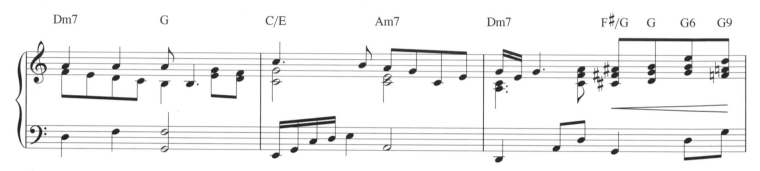

CHRISTINE:

RAOUL: An-y-where you go, let me go

f

ff largo

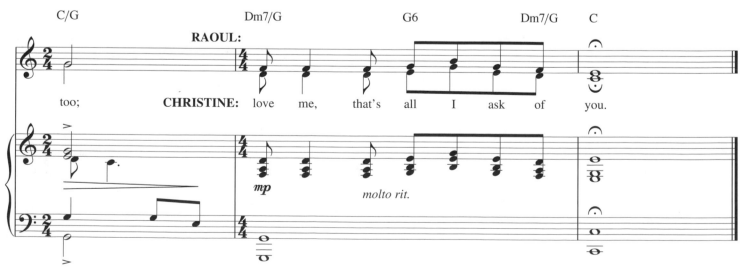

RAOUL:

too; **CHRISTINE:** love me, that's all I ask of you.

mp *molto rit.*

And This Is My Beloved

from KISMET

Words and Music by
Robert Wright and George Forrest
(Music based on themes of A. Borodin)

sift - ing; I - mag - ine these _____ on one ea - ger mouth,

Poco più mosso

And this is my be - lov - ed. And when he speaks,

And when he talks to me, Mu - sic! Mys - ter-y!

And when he moves And when he walks with me, Par - a - dise _____ comes sud - den - ly

Poco stentato

near!

All that can stir,

All that can stun,

All that's for the heart's lift - ing;

I - mag - ine these _____ in

one per-fect one, _____

And this is my be - lov - ed! _____

_____ And this is my be - lov - ed! _____

The Greatest of These

from PHILEMON

Words and Music by Tom Jones
and Harvey Schmidt

Simply (♩ = 104)

Though I speak with the tongues of men and an - gels and have not love, and have not love; Though I'm blessed with the spe - cial gift of proph - e - cy, and have not love, and have not

With pedal

love;   Though my faith is strong e - nough to move a

moun - tain.   Though I be - stow my world - ly goods to feed the

poor.   Though my bod - y may be

tor - tured,   if I have not lived with love   I am

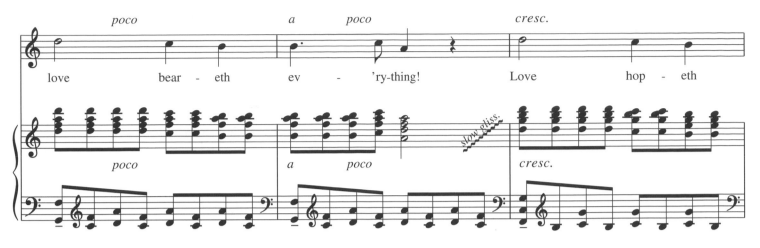

poco   *a*   *poco*   *cresc.*

love   bear - eth   ev - 'ry-thing!   Love   hop - eth

poco   *a poco*   *cresc.*

Broader

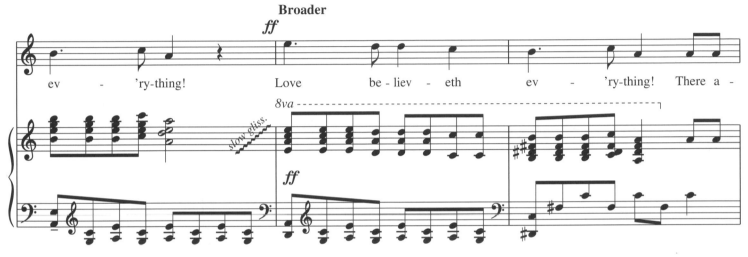

ff

ev - 'ry-thing!   Love   be - liev - eth   ev - 'ry-thing!   There a -

ff

mp   *p*

bid - eth three things: Faith,   hope and love.   But the

mf   *mp*   *p*

great - est of these   is   love

pp   *rit.*   *p a tempo*

More I Cannot Wish You

from GUYS AND DOLLS

By Frank Loesser

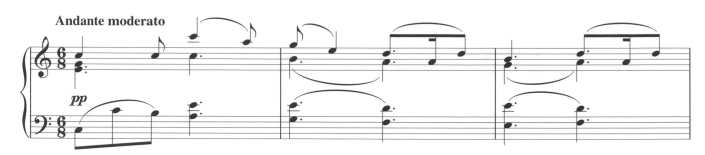

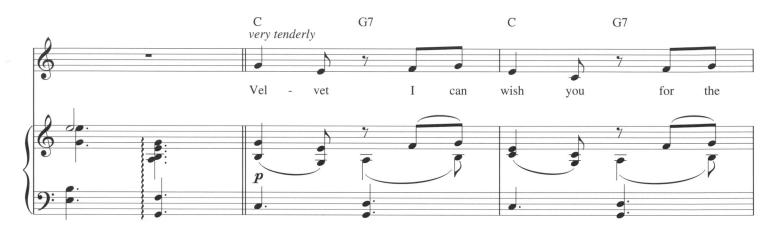

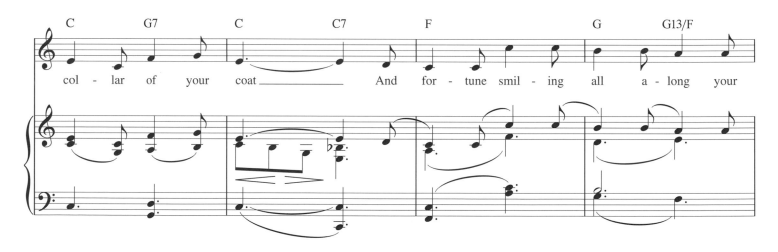

wish you find your love, _____ Your own true love, _____ this

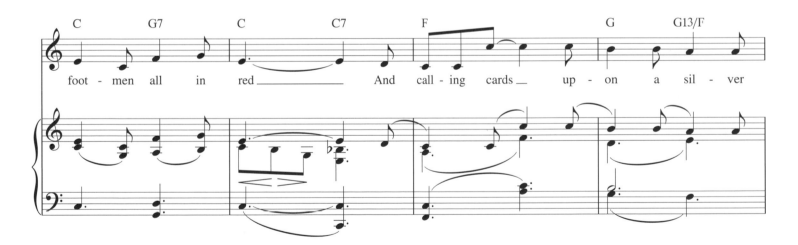

day _____ Man - sions I can wish you sev - en

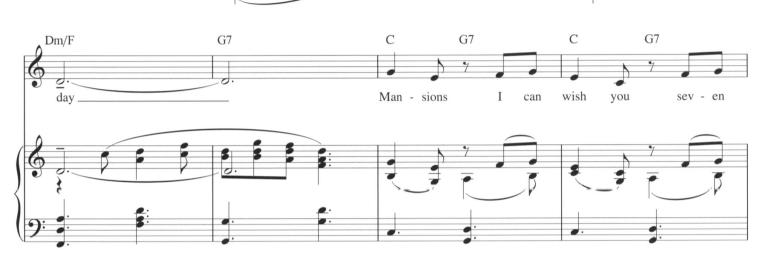

foot - men all in red _____ And call - ing cards _ up - on a sil - ver

tray _____ But more I can - not wish _ you than to

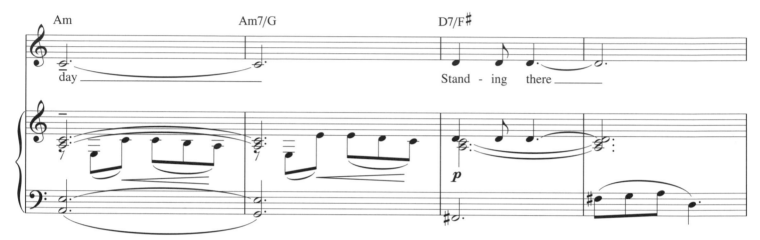

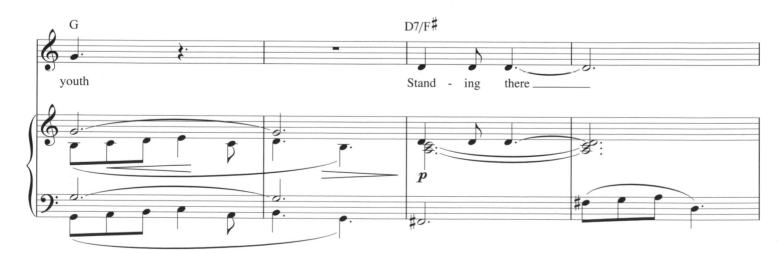

wish you find your love, _____ Your own true love, _____ this

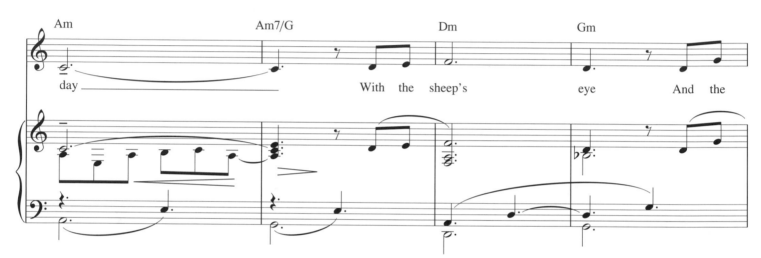

day _____ With the sheep's eye And the

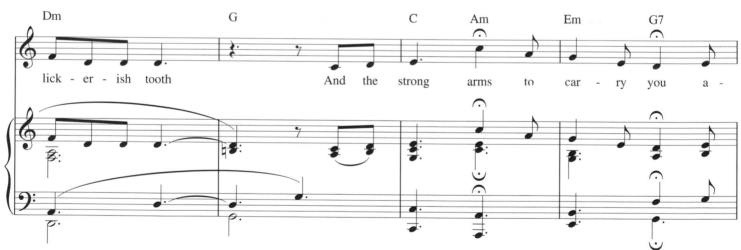

lick - er - ish tooth And the strong arms to car - ry you a -

way.

Sunrise, Sunset

from the Musical FIDDLER ON THE ROOF

Words by Sheldon Harnick
Music by Jerry Bock

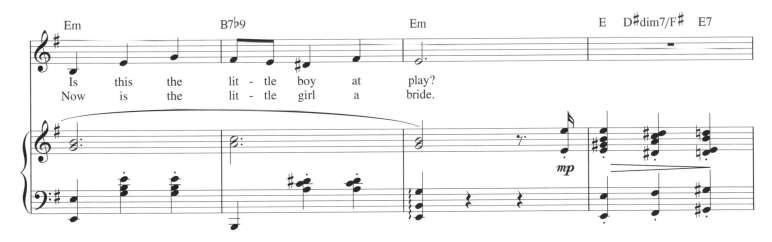

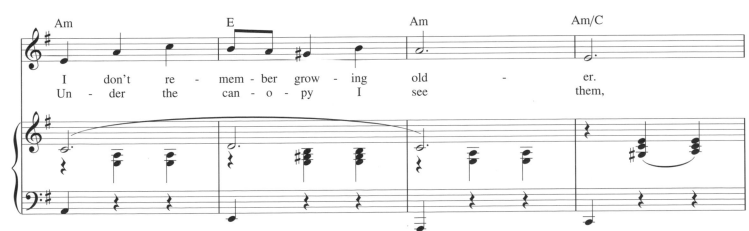

Blos - som - ing e - ven as we gaze.

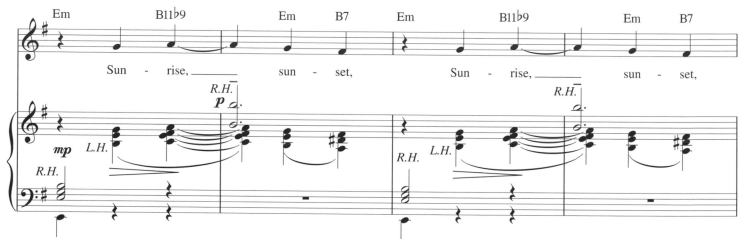

Sun - rise, _____ sun - set, Sun - rise, _____ sun - set,

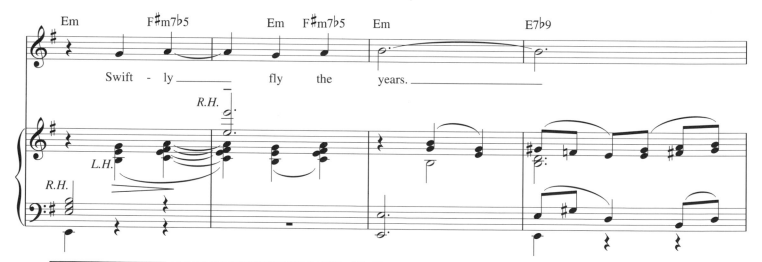

Swift - ly _____ fly the years. _____

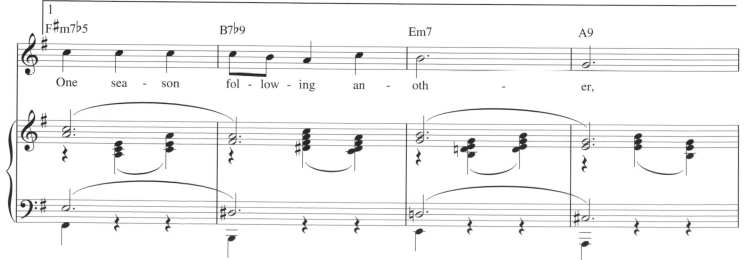

One sea - son fol - low - ing an - oth - er,

Some Enchanted Evening

from SOUTH PACIFIC

Lyrics by Oscar Hammerstein II
Music by Richard Rodgers

Someone Like You

from *JEKYLL & HYDE*

Words by Leslie Bricusse
Music by Frank Wildhorn

Slowly, with expression

I peered through win-dows,   watched life go by.   Dreamed of to-mor-row,
It's like you took my dreams,   made each one real.   You reached in-side of me

but stayed in - side.   The past was hold - ing me,
and made me feel.   And now I see a world

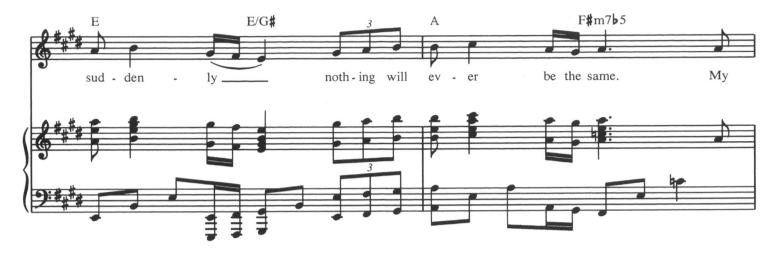

sud-den-ly _____ noth-ing will ev-er be the same. My

heart's tak-en wing, _ and I feel so a-live, _____ 'cause

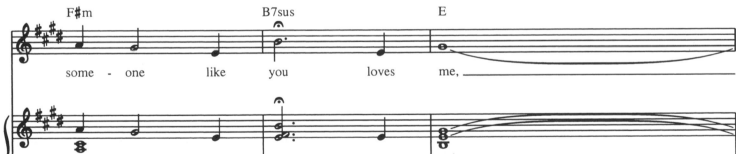

some-one like you loves me, _____

Till There Was You

from Meredith Willson's THE MUSIC MAN

By Meredith Willson

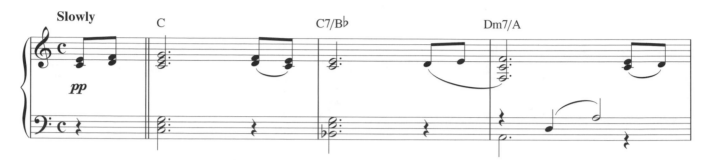

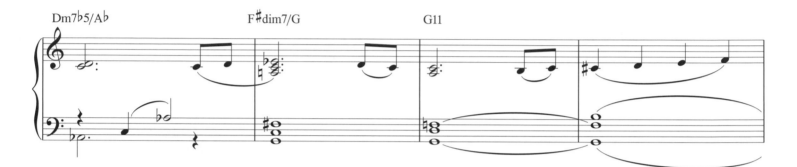

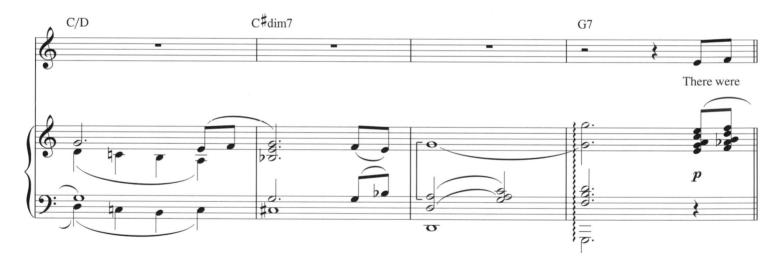

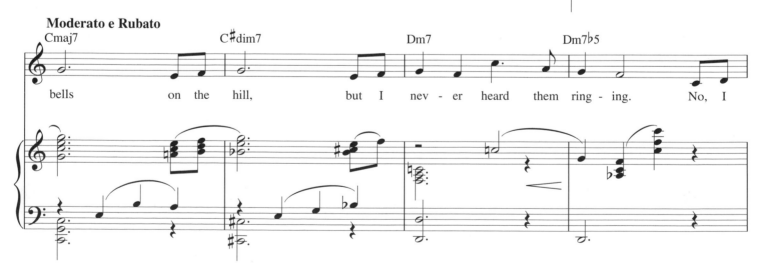

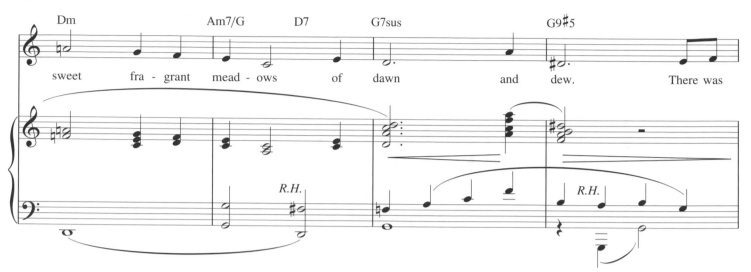

sweet fra - grant mead - ows of dawn and dew. There was

love all a - round, but I nev - er heard it sing - ing. No, I

nev - er heard it at all, till there was you. _____

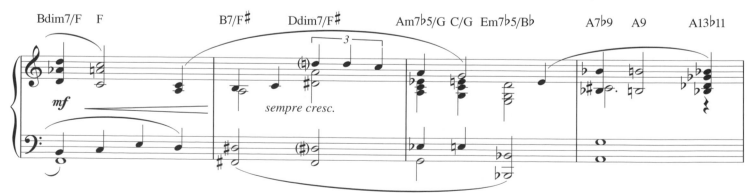

Unexpected Song
from SONG & DANCE

Music by Andrew Lloyd Webber
Lyrics by Don Black

Gently (♩=76)

C   **Dm/C**   **G/C**

I have nev-er felt like this, for once I'm lost for
I don't know what's go-ing on, can't work it out at

Am   **Am/G**   **G/F**   **F**   **F/G**

words, your smile has real-ly thrown me.
all. What-ev-er made you choose me?

C   **Dm/C**   **G/C**

This is not like me at all, I nev-er thought I'd
I just can't be-lieve my eyes, you look at me as

song that on-ly we are hear - ing.   hear - ing.

I have nev - er felt like this.   For once I'm lost for

words,   your smile has real - ly thrown me.

This   is not like me at all;   I nev - er thought I'd

know   the kind of love you've shown me.

Now   no mat - ter where I am,   no mat - ter what I

do,   I see your face ap - pear - ing

like   an un - ex - pect - ed song,   an un - ex - pect - ed

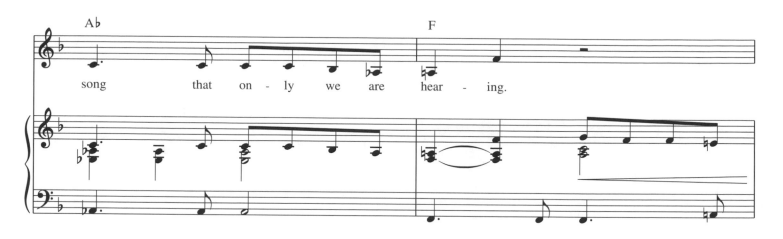

song that on - ly we are hear - ing.

Like an un - ex - pect - ed song, an un - ex - pect - ed

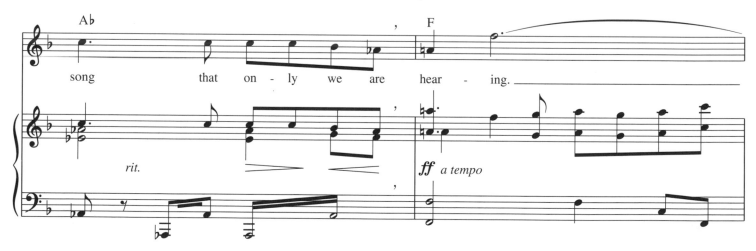

song that on - ly we are hear - ing.

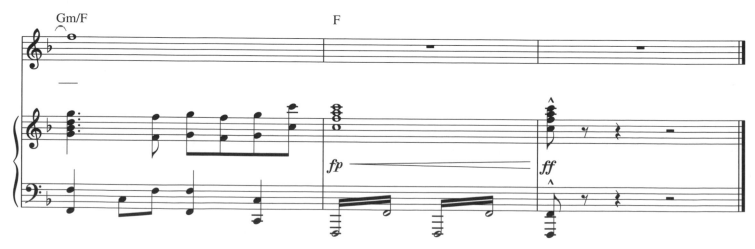

All the Way
from the film THE JOKER IS WILD

Words by Sammy Cahn
Music by James Van Heusen
Arranged by Hank Powell

way. Tall - er_____ than the tall - est tree is, that's how it's got to

feel. Deep - er_____ than the deep blue sea is, that's how deep it goes,_ if it's

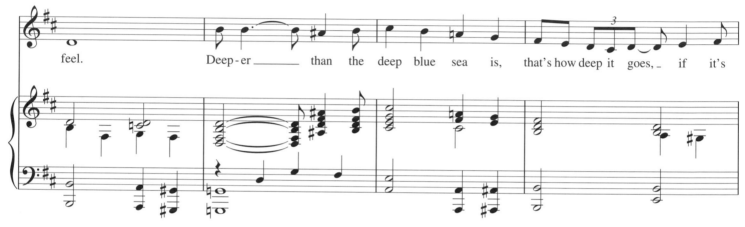

real. When some-bod - y needs you, it's no good un - less { he / she } needs you

all the way. Through the good or lean years and for

all the in - be - tween years, come what may.

Who knows where the road will lead us, on - ly a fool would say. But

if you let me love you, it's for sure I'm gon - na love you all the way,

all the way.

espressivo

rit.

pp

8vb

Fly Me to the Moon
(In Other Words)

Words and Music by
Bart Howard
Arranged by Hank Powell

Gently, slowly

Fly me to the moon, and let me play a - mong the stars;

Let me see what spring is like on Ju - pit - er and Mars. In

oth - er words: _____ hold my hand. In oth - er words: _____

darling, kiss me. Fill my heart with

song, and let me sing for-ev-er-more. You are all I

long for, all I wor - ship and a - dore. In oth - er words: please be

true. In oth - er words: I love you.

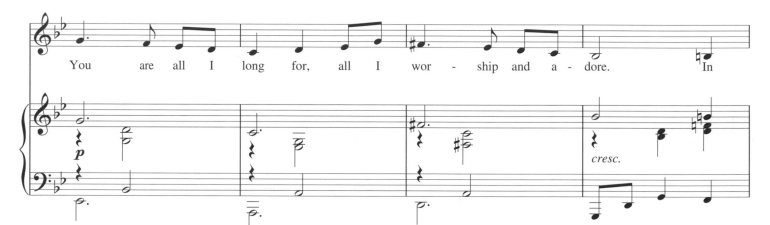

You are all I long for, all I wor - ship and a - dore. In

oth - er words: _____ please be true. _____ In oth - er words:

I love you. _____

I Could Write a Book

from PAL JOEY

Words by Lorenz Hart
Music by Richard Rodgers
Arranged by Brian Dean

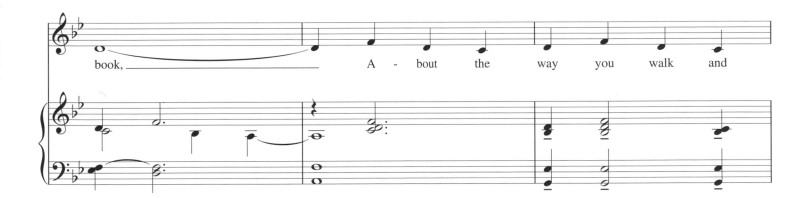

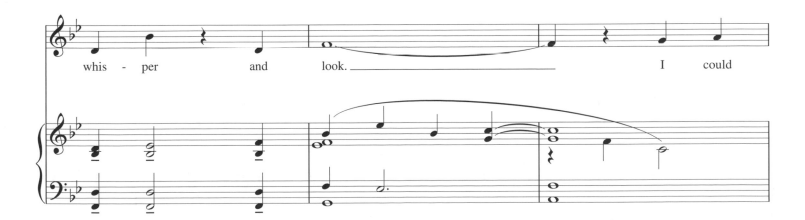

lot. _____ Then the world dis -

cov - ers as my book ends, how to make two

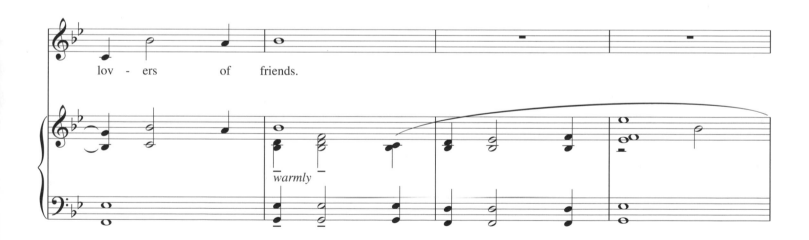

lov - ers of friends.

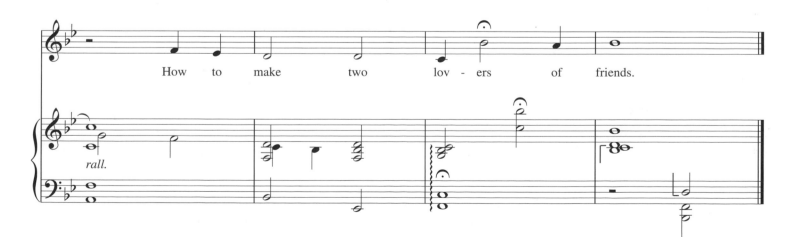

How to make two lov - ers of friends.

Let It Be Me
(Je T'appartiens)

English Words by Mann Curtis
French Words by Pierre DeLanoe
Music by Gilbert Becaud
Arranged by John Reed

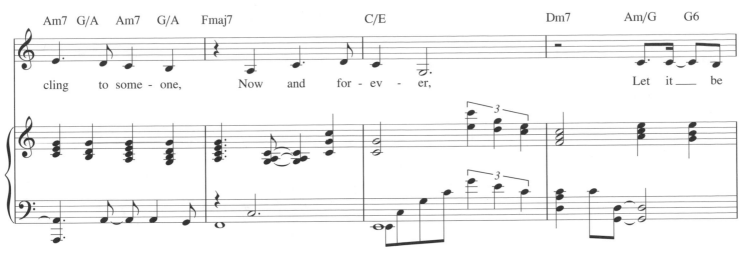

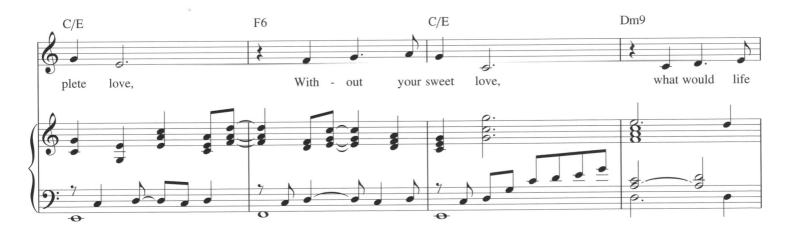

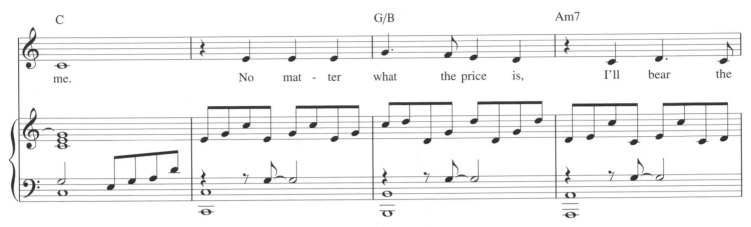

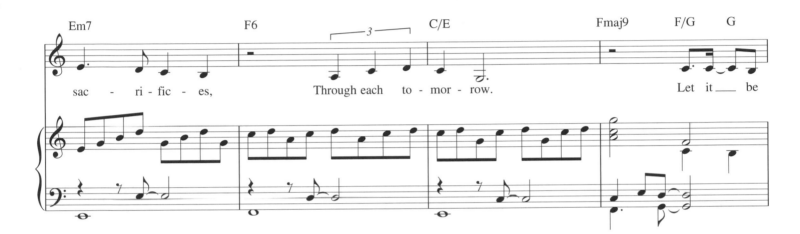

The Promise
(I'll Never Say Goodbye)
Theme from the Universal Motion Picture THE PROMISE

Words by Alan and Marilyn Bergman
Music by David Shire

mor - row   as   much   as   to - day. _____   I   am   not   a -

fraid   to   say,   "I   love   you," _____   and   I   prom-ise   you   I'll

nev - er   say   "good - bye."

How   could   I   ev - er   say   "good - bye?"

*Cue notes optional 2nd time

Starting Here, Starting Now

Words by Richard Maltby Jr.
Music by David Shire

Quite slowly, with a steady beat

Time After Time

from the Metro-Goldwyn-Mayer Picture IT HAPPENED IN BROOKLYN

Words by Sammy Cahn
Music by Jule Styne
Arranged by Richard Walters

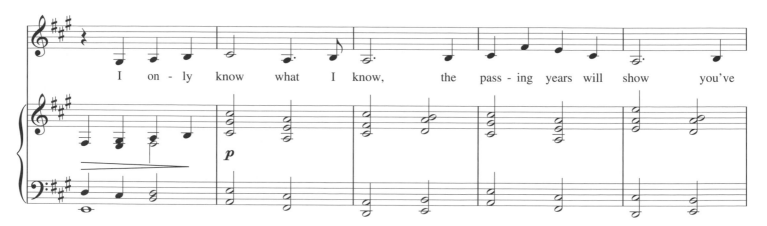

I on - ly know what I know, the pass - ing years will show you've

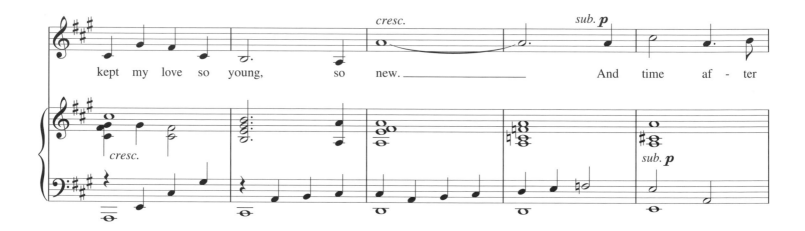

kept my love so young, so new._____ And time af - ter

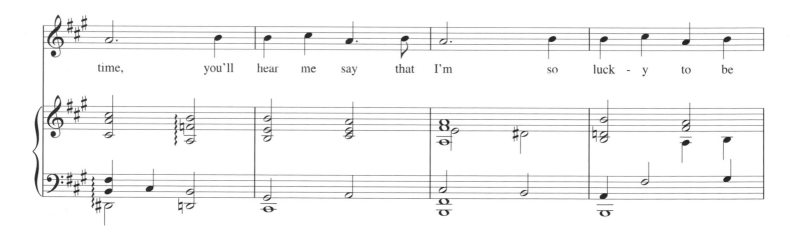

time, you'll hear me say that I'm so luck - y to be

lov - ing you. I on - ly know what I

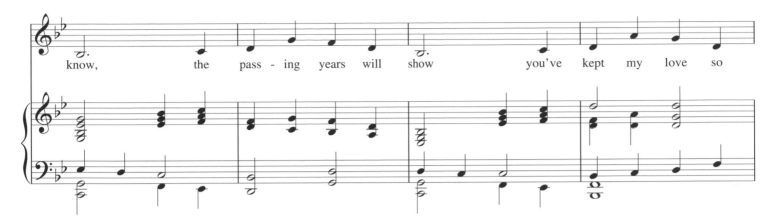

know, the pass - ing years will show you've kept my love so

young, so new. _____ And time af - ter

time, you'll hear me say that I'm so luck - y to be

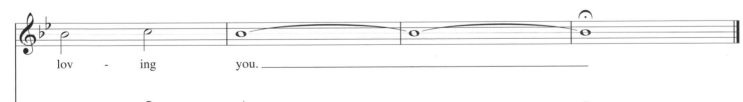

lov - ing you. _____

Walk Hand in Hand

Words and Music by
Johnny Cowell
Arranged by Joel K. Boyd

Lyrics: Walk hand in hand with me through all e- ter - ni - ty, have faith, be - lieve in me, give me your hand. Love is a

sym - pho - ny of per - fect har - mo - ny,

when lov - ers such as we walk hand in

hand. Be not a - fraid, for

I am with you all the while. So lift _____ your head up

high _____ and look _____ to - ward the sky!

Walk hand in hand with me, God is our

des - ti - ny, no great - er love could be, walk hand in

hand, walk with me.

The Way You Look Tonight
from SWING TIME

Words by Dorothy Fields
Music by Jerome Kern
Arranged by Hank Powell

Some - day when I'm aw - f'ly low,
love - ly, with your smile so warm,

when the world is cold, I will feel a glow just think - ing of
and your cheek so soft, there is noth - ing for me but to love

you and the way you look to - night.
you just the way you look to -

Oh, but you're

night. With each word your

ten - der - ness grows, _____ tear - ing my fear _____ a -

part, _____ and that laugh that wrink les your nose _____

_____ touch - es my fool - ish heart. _____

poco cresc.

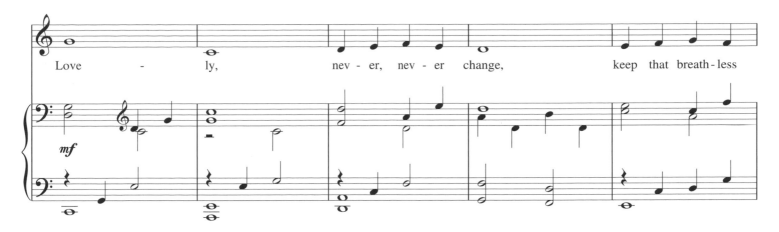

Love - ly, nev - er, nev - er change, keep that breath - less

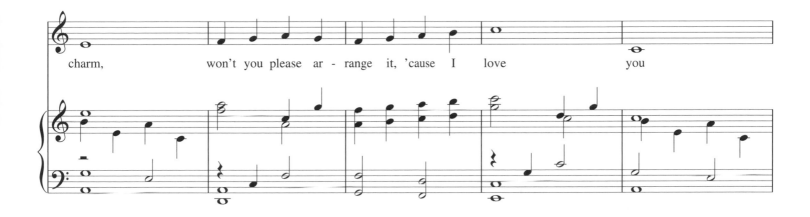

charm, won't you please ar - range it, 'cause I love you

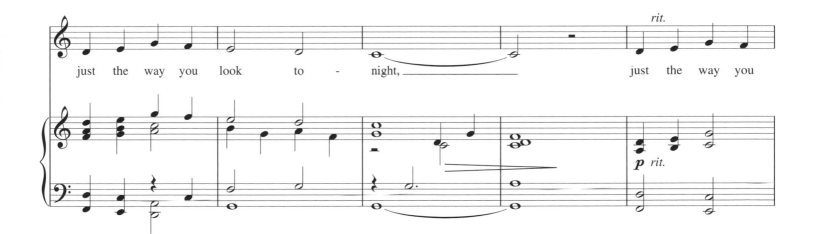

just the way you look to - night, _____ just the way you

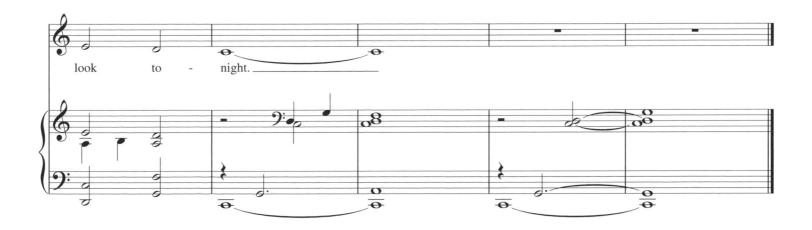

look to - night. _____

With a Song in My Heart

from SPRING IS HERE

Words by Lorenz Hart
Music by Richard Rodgers
Arranged by Richard Walters

hand; It tells that you're stand - ing near,

and At the sound of your voice Heav - en o - pens its

por - tals to me. Can I help but re - joice

That a song such as ours came to be? But I al - ways knew

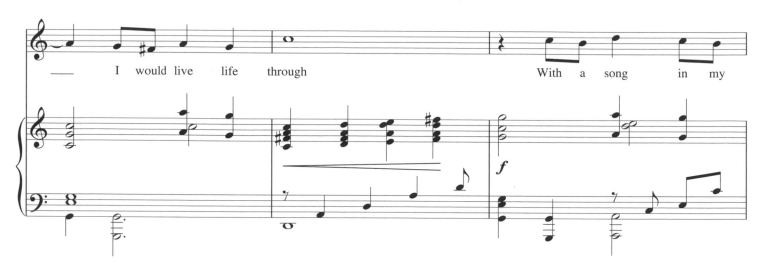

I would live life through With a song in my

heart for you.

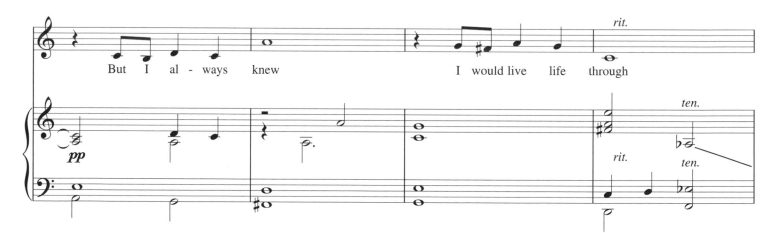

But I al - ways knew I would live life through

Slowly to the end

With a song in my heart for you.

Annie's Song
Recorded by John Denver

Words and Music by John Denver
Arranged by Richard Walters

Moderately fast; flowing

You fill up my

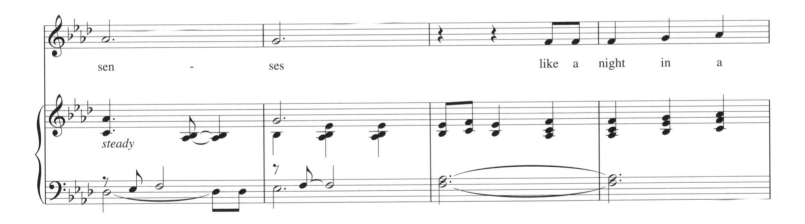

sen - ses like a night in a
steady

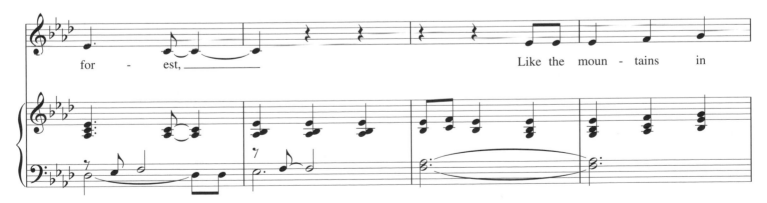

for - est, _____ Like the moun - tains in

spring - time, _____ like a walk in the rain, _

_____ Like a storm in the __

des - ert, like a sleep - y blue

o - cean, _____ You fill up my __

sen - ses, come fill me a -

gain.

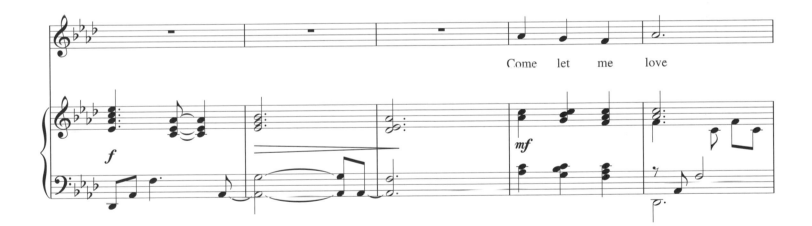

Come let me love you,

you, let me give my life to

you, _____ Let me drown in your laugh -

ter, let me die in your arms, _____

Let me

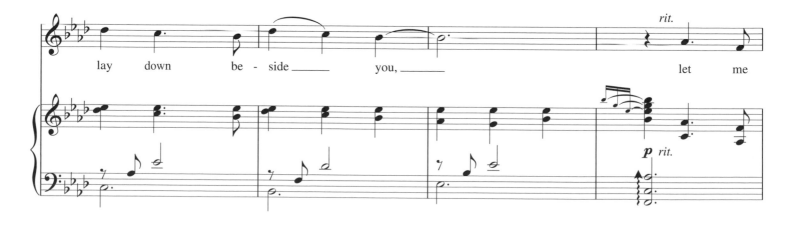

lay down be - side _____ you, _____ let me

al - ways be with you,_____ come _

__ let me love _____ you, come

love me a - gain._____

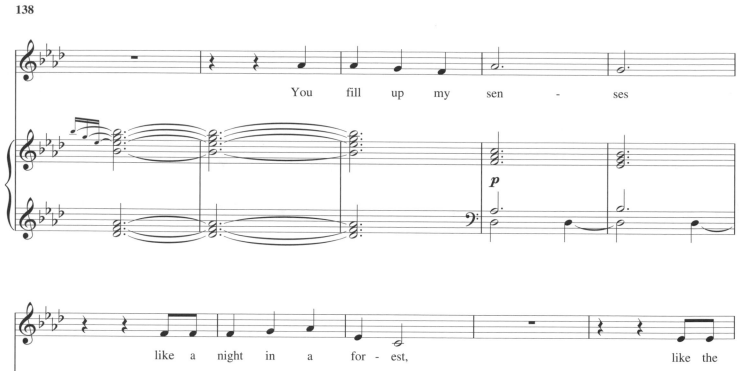

You fill up my sen - ses

like a night in a for - est,   like the

moun - tains in spring - time,   like a walk in the

rain, _____   like a storm in the des -

ert, like a sleep - y blue o - cean, ___

you fill up my sen - ses,

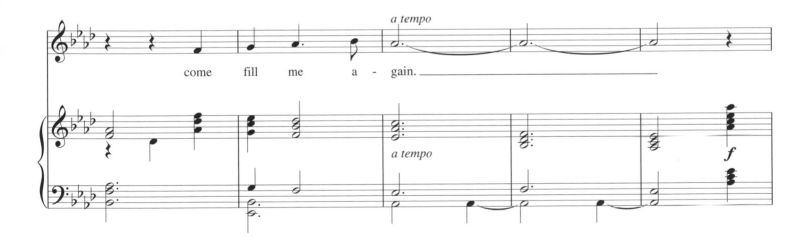

come fill me a - gain. ___

Endless Love
Recorded by Lionel Richie

Words and Music by
Lionel Richie

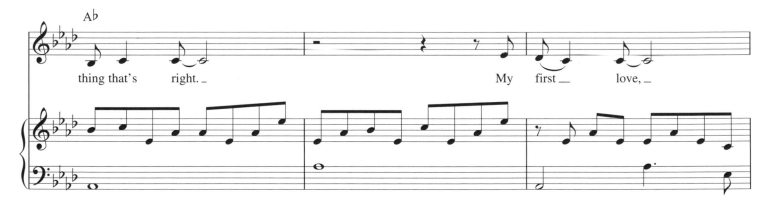

step I make. And I,

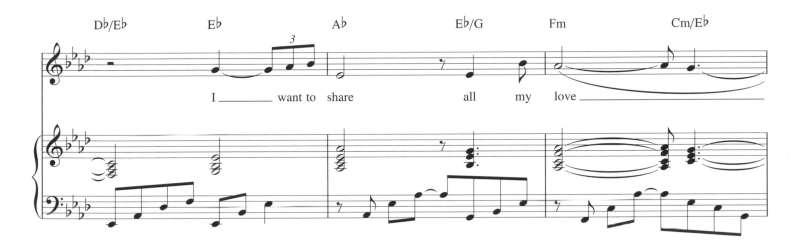

I ____ want to share all my love ____

____ with you, no one else ____ will ____ do. ____

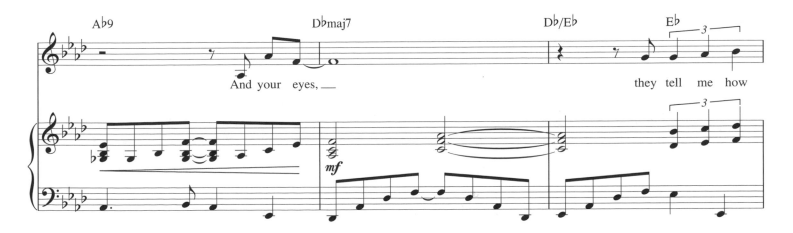

And your eyes, ____ they tell me how

much you — care. _____ Oh, _____ yes, you will

al - ways be my end - less

love. _____

Two hearts, _ two hearts that

beat as _ one; _ our lives have just be - gun. _

For - ev - er, _ I'll hold you

close in my arms, _ I can't re - sist your charms. _

And love, I'll be a

fool   for   you _____ I'm _____ sure;

You _ know   I don't   mind. _____   'Cause you, _

_____ you mean the world   to ___ me. _____

_____   Oh,   I know   I've found _____ in

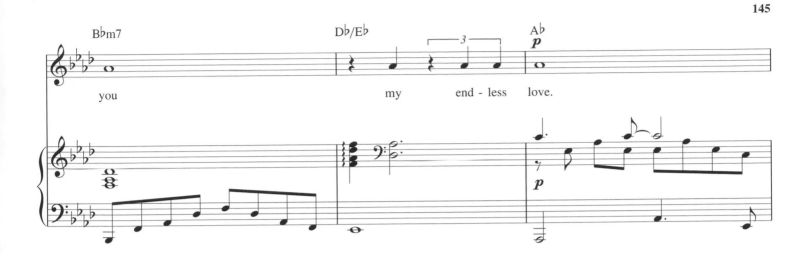

you my end - less love.

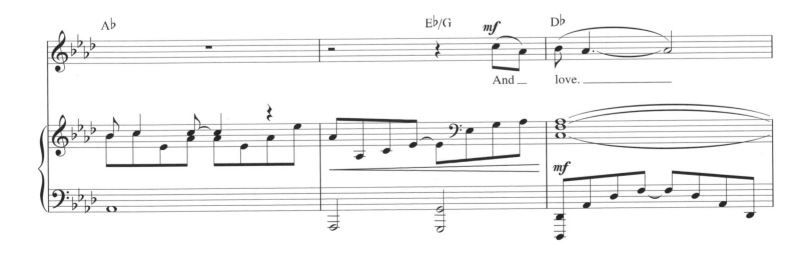

And — love.

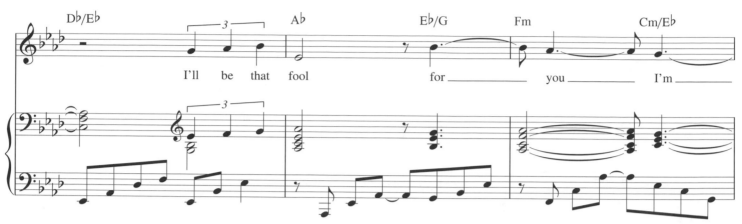

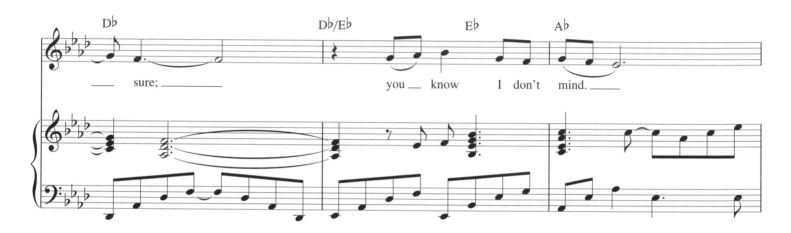

this love _____ I have in - side.   I'll

give _____ it all to you   my love, _ my love, _

_ my end - less love.

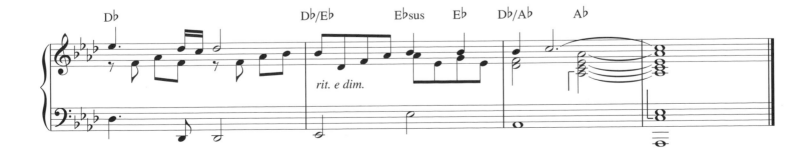

Grow Old with Me

Recorded by John Lennon

Words and Music by
John Lennon

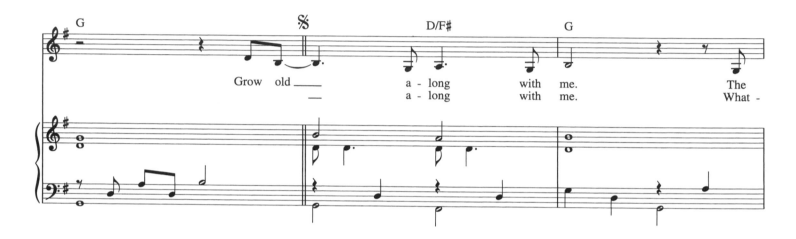

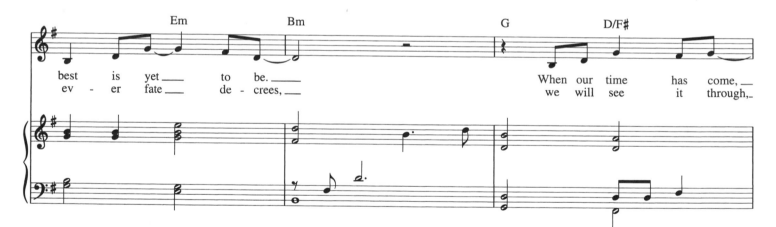

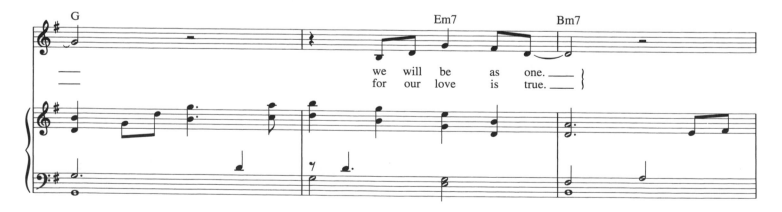

God bless our love. God bless our __

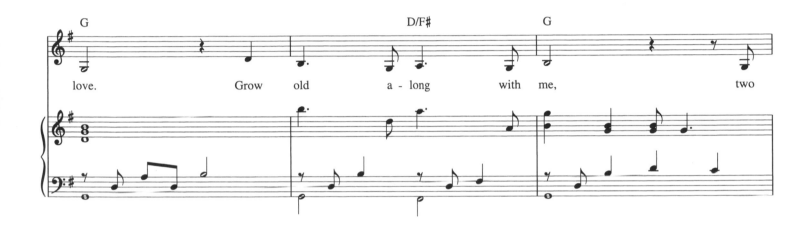

love. Grow old a - long with me, two

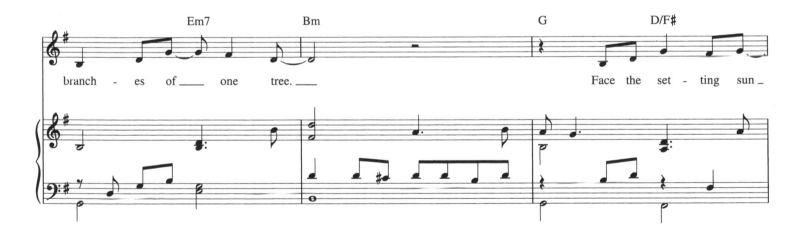

branch - es of ___ one tree. ___ Face the set - ting sun __

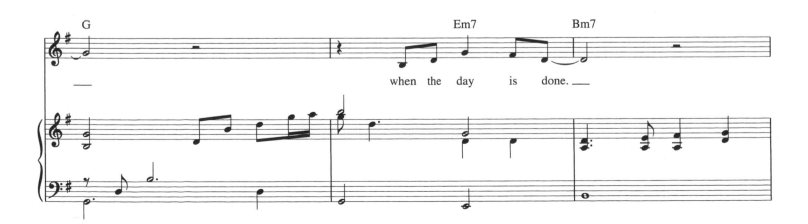

___ when the day is done. ___

God bless our love.   God bless our __

love.   Spend-ing our lives ___ to - geth - er,

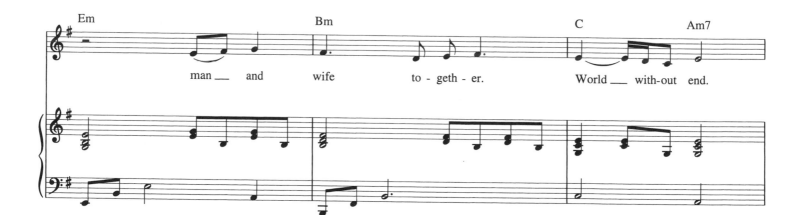

man __ and wife   to - geth - er.   World __ with-out end.

World _____ with-out end.

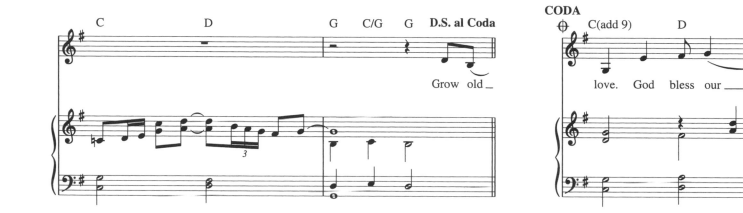

Grow old __ love. God bless our _____

love. God bless our __ love.

Here, There and Everywhere

Recorded by The Beatles

Words and Music by John Lennon
and Paul McCartney

I Will

Recorded by The Beatles

Words and Music by John Lennon
and Paul McCartney

-er real - ly mat - tered; I will al - ways feel __ the same. __

Love you for - ev - er and __ for - ev - er, love you with all __ my heart. __

__ Love you when - ev - er we're __ to - geth - er,

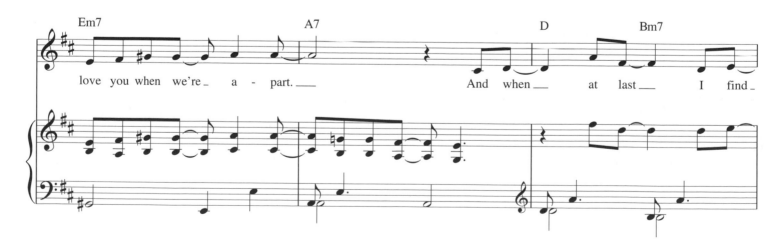

love you when we're __ a - part. __ And when __ at last __ I find __

you, ___ your song ___ will fill ___ the air. ___ Sing it loud ___ so I ___ can hear ___

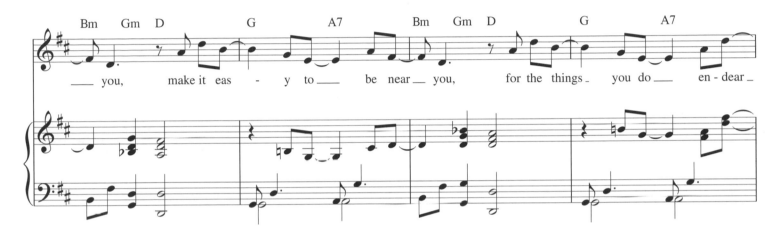

___ you, make it eas - y to ___ be near ___ you, for the things ___ you do ___ en - dear ___

___ you to ___ me. Ah, ___ you know ___ I will. ___ I

will. _____

In My Life

Recorded by The Beatles

Words and Music by John Lennon
and Paul McCartney
Arranged by John Reed

Lyrically, not too slow

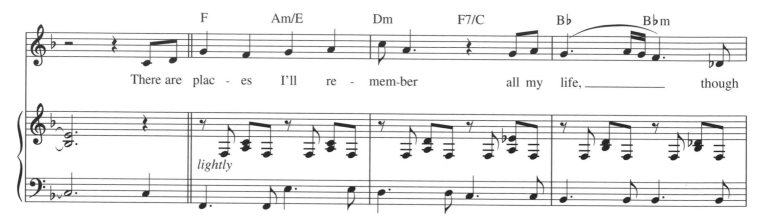

There are plac - es I'll re - mem - ber all my life, _____ though

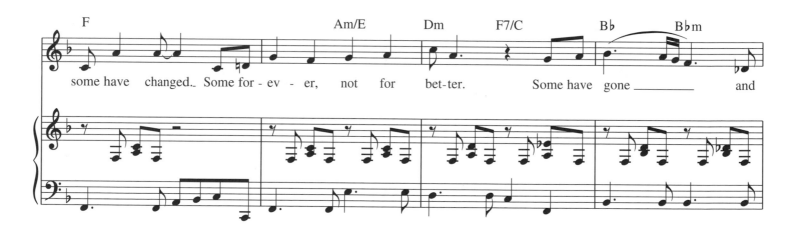

some have changed._ Some for - ev - er, not for bet - ter. Some have gone _____ and

some re - mained._ All those plac - es _ have _ their _ mo - ments with lov - ers and friends _ I

went be-fore, ___ I know I'll of-ten stop and think a-bout them. In my ___ life, I love you more. ___

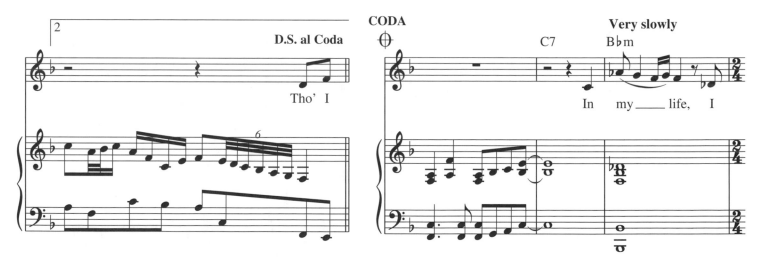

Tho' I

In my ___ life, I

love you more.

We've Only Just Begun

Recorded by The Carpenters

Words and Music by Roger Nichols
and Paul Williams

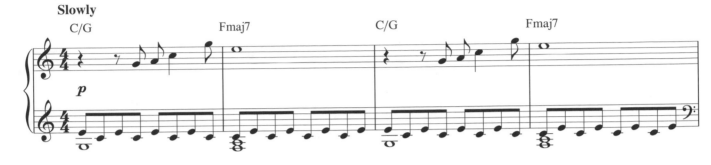

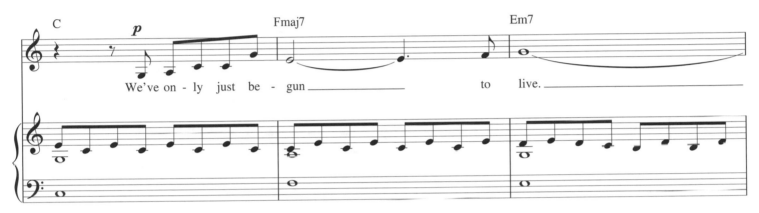

We've on-ly just be-gun _____ to live. _____

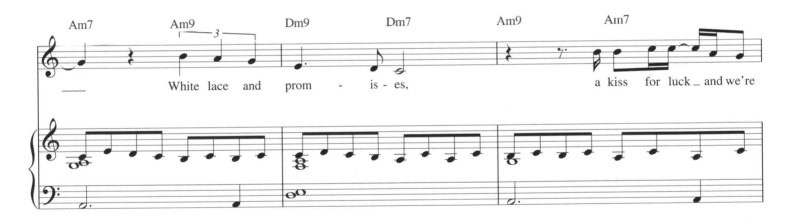

_____ White lace and prom - is - es, a kiss for luck _ and we're

on our way. _____

(1.) Be - fore the ris - ing
(2.) And when the eve - ning

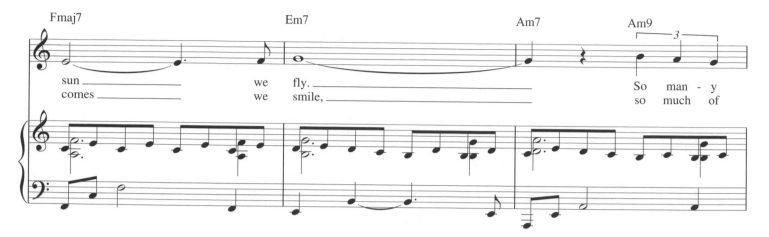

sun _____ we fly. _____
comes _____ we smile, _____

So man-y
so much of

roads to choose,
life a-head,

we start out walk-ing and learn to run. _____
we'll find a place where there's room to grow. _____

To Coda

And yes, we've just be-gun. _____

Shar-ing ho-ri-zons that are new to us,

watch-ing the signs a-long the

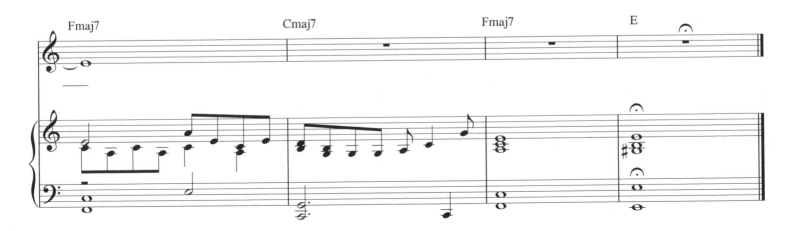

You Are So Beautiful

Recorded by Joe Cocker

Words and Music by Billy Preston
and Bruce Fisher

Moderately slow, expressively

You are so __

beau-ti - ful __ to

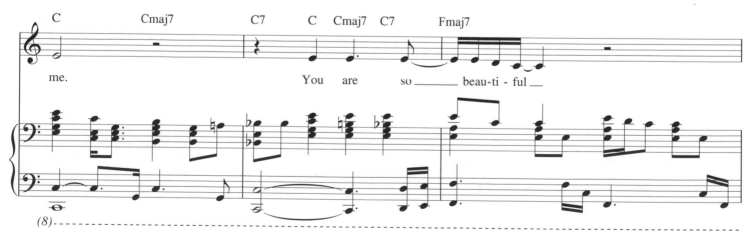

me.

You are so __ beau-ti - ful __

You Raise Me Up

Recorded by Josh Groban

Words and Music by Brendan Graham
and Rolf Lovland

Moderately slow

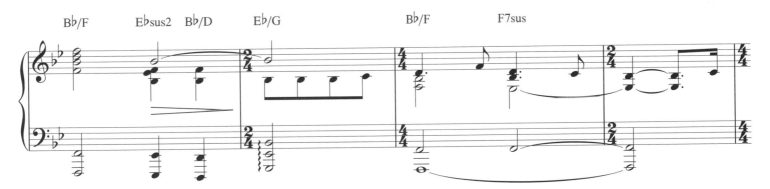

When I am down ___ and oh, my soul's so

wea - ry, when trou-bles come and my heart _ bur-dened be, then I am

still ___ and wait here in the si - lence un - til you come and sit a while _ with

me. You raise me up so I can stand on moun - tains. You raise me

up to walk on storm - y seas. I am strong ___ when I am on ___ your _

shoul - ders. You raise me up to more than I ____ can be.

You raise me up so I can stand on moun - tains. You raise me

up to walk on storm - y seas. I am strong when I am on ___ your

shoul - ders. You raise me up to more than I ___ can ___ be.

You raise me up so I can stand ___ on moun - tains. You raise me

up to walk on storm - y seas. I ___ am ___ strong ___ when I am on ___ your

This repeat may be omitted.

How Beautiful

Recorded by Twila Paris

Words and Music by
Twila Paris

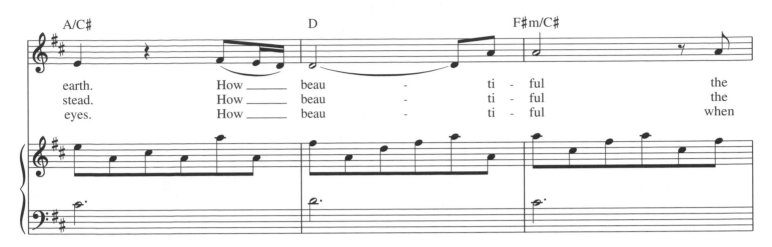

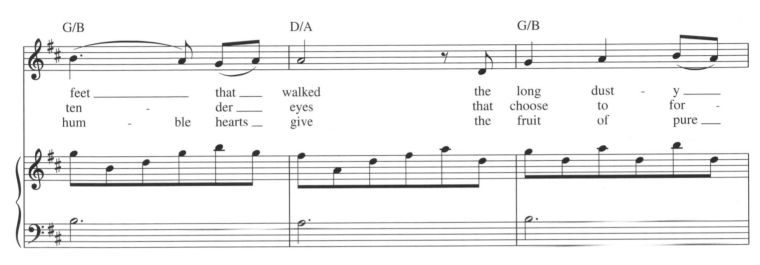

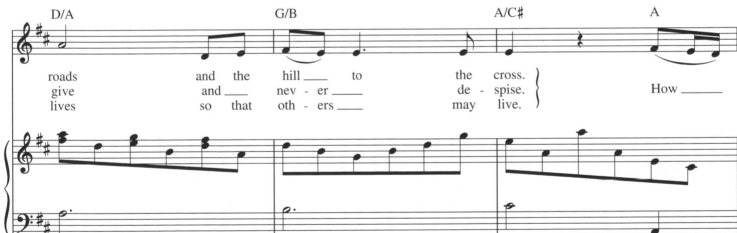

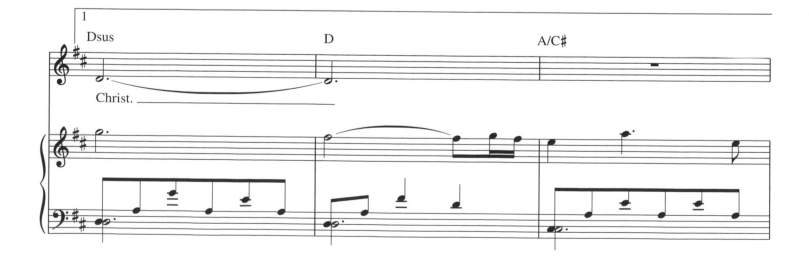

How Christ. And as He laid

down His life, we of - fer ___ this

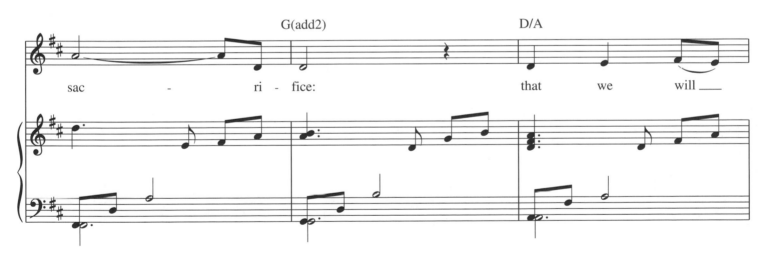

sac - ri - fice: that we will ___

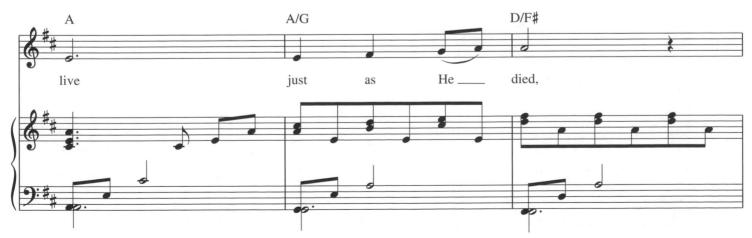

live just as He ___ died,

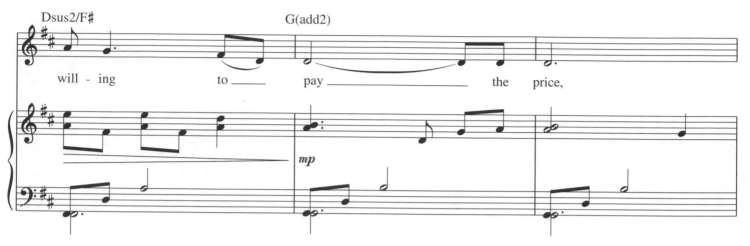

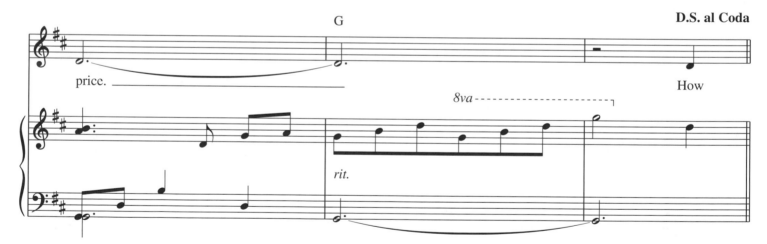

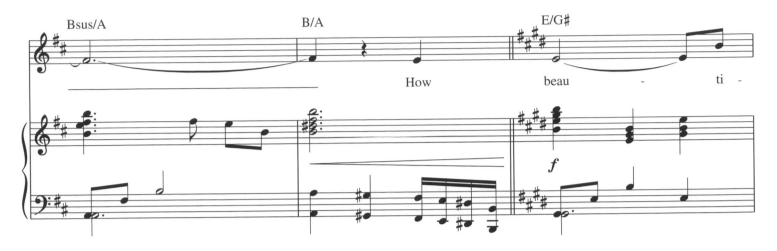

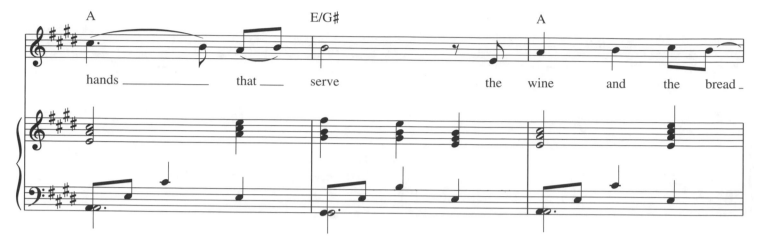

hands _____ that ____ serve the wine and the bread ___

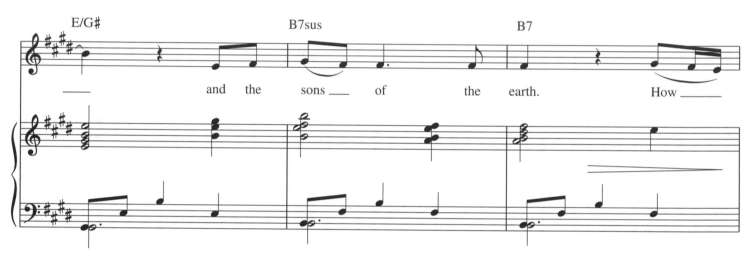

___ and the sons ___ of the earth. How _____

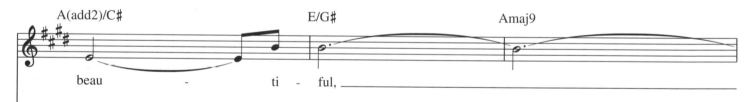

beau - ti - ful, _____

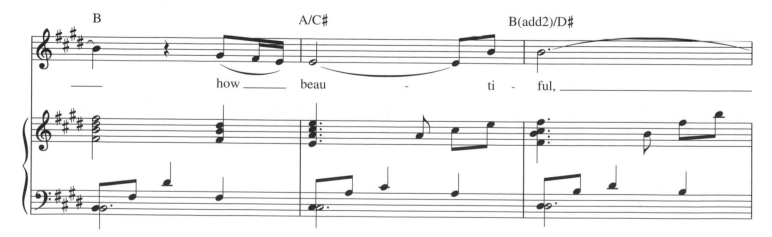

___ how ____ beau - ti - ful, _____

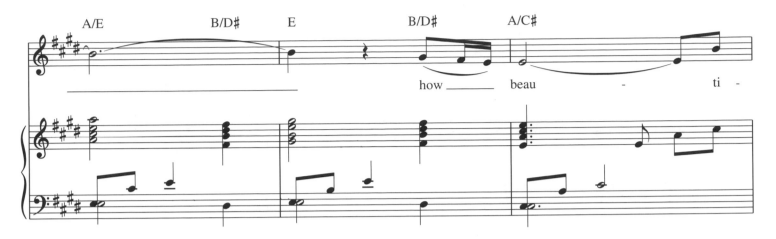

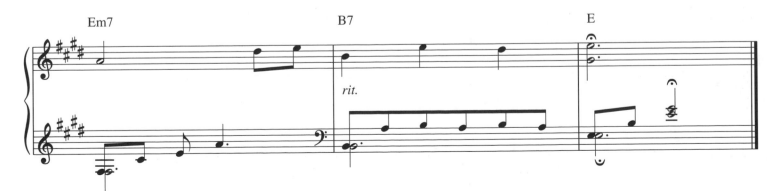

I Will Be Here

Recorded by Steven Curtis Chapman

Words and Music by
Steven Curtis Chapman

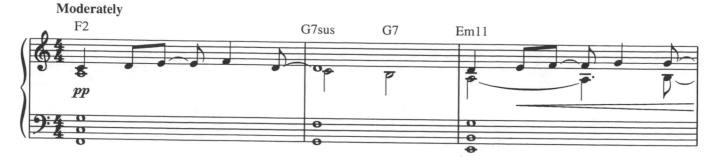

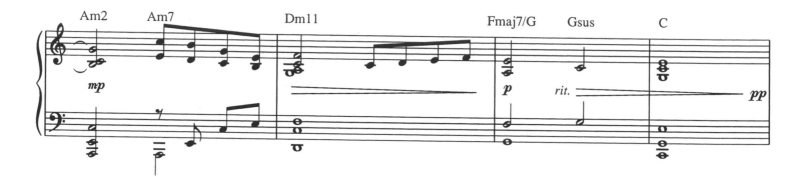

To-mor-row morn-in' if you ___ wake up and the sun does ___ not ___ ap - pear,___
To-mor-row morn-in' if you ___ wake up and the fu - ture is ___ un - clear,___

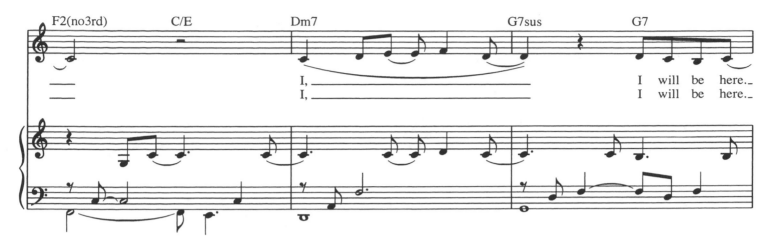

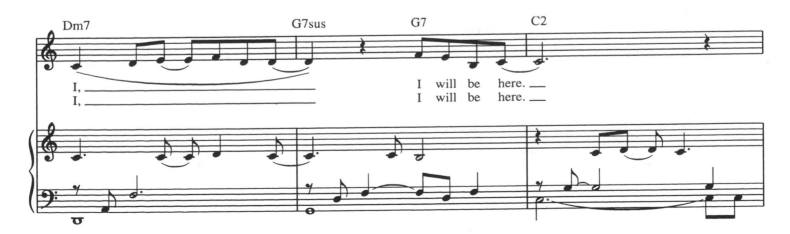

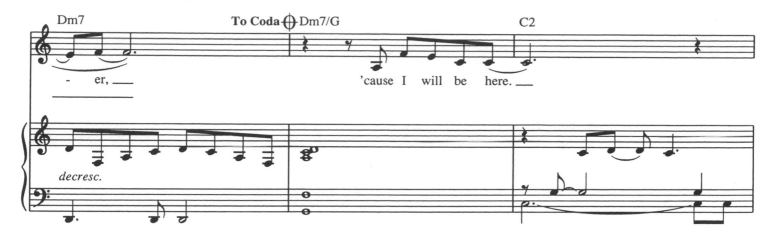

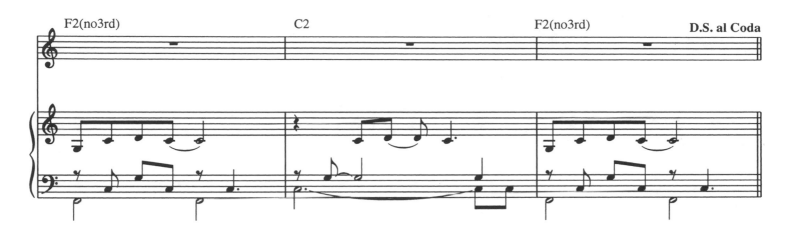

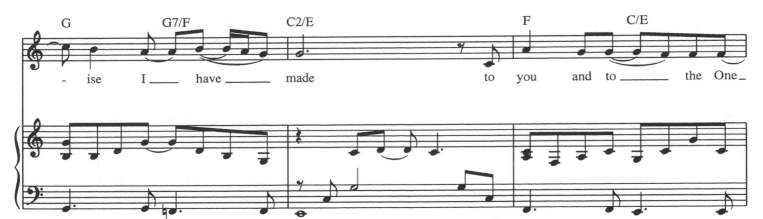

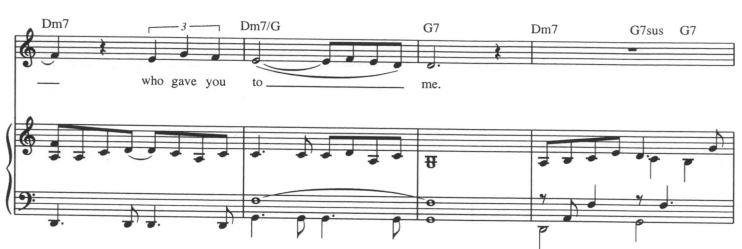

who gave you to _____ me.

I, _____ I will be here. __

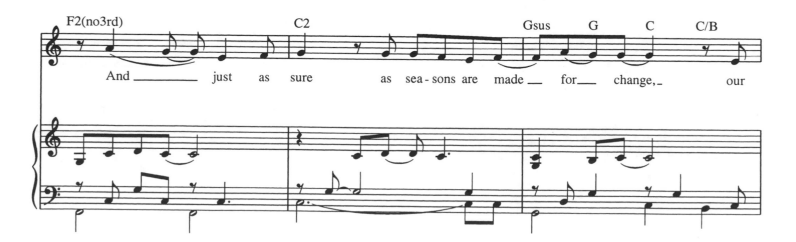

And _____ just as sure as sea-sons are made __ for __ change, __ our

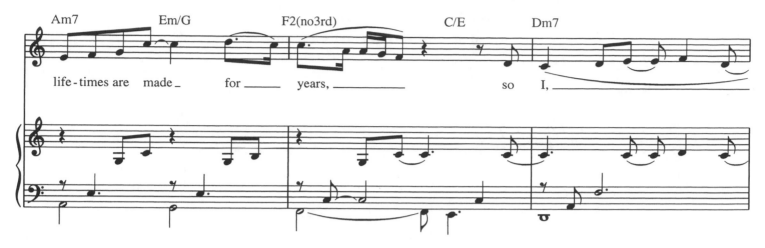

life-times are made __ for ____ years, _____ so I, ____

I _____ will be __ here. ____ We'll be to-geth-er. __

I will be __ here. __

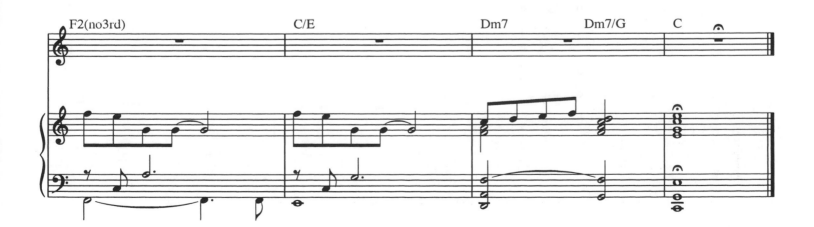

If You Could See What I See

Recorded by Steven Curtis Chapman

Words and Music by Geoff Moore
and Steven Curtis Chapman

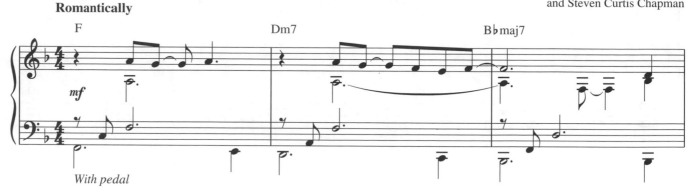

All of my life __
I know there are days __

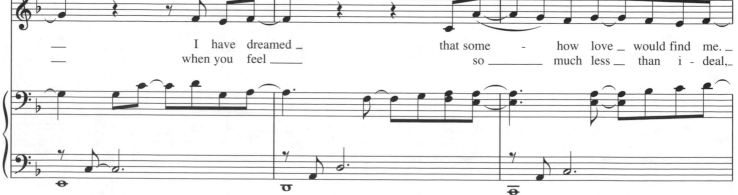

I have dreamed __ that some - how love __ would find me. __
when you feel _____ so _____ much less __ than i - deal,

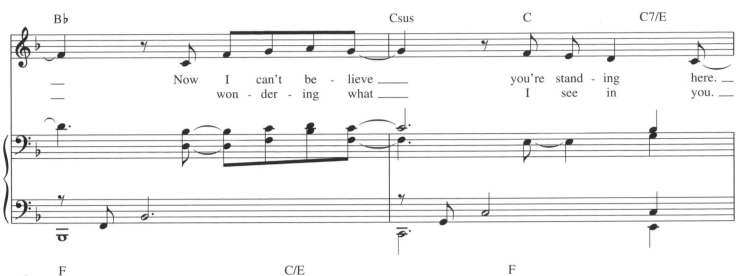

Now I can't be - lieve _____ you're stand - ing here. _____
won - der - ing what _____ I see in you. _____

_____ If beau - ty is all _____
_____ It's all of the light _____

_____ in the eye _____ of _____ the be - hold - er, then I _____
_____ and the grace; _____ your be - lief _____ in me drives _ me to say _____

_____ wish you could see _____ the love _____ for you _ that lives _
that I prom - ise you _____ a faith - ful love, _ for - ev -

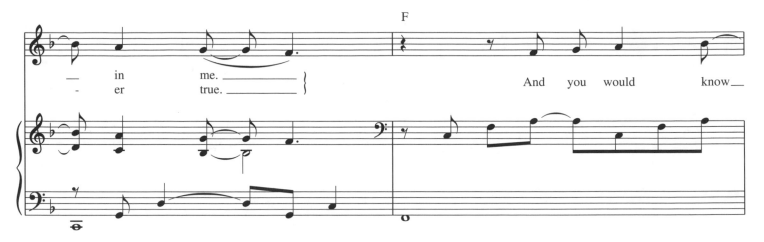

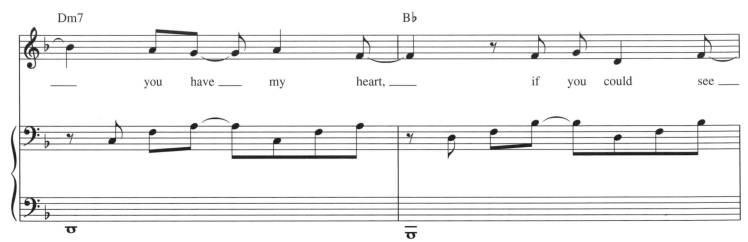

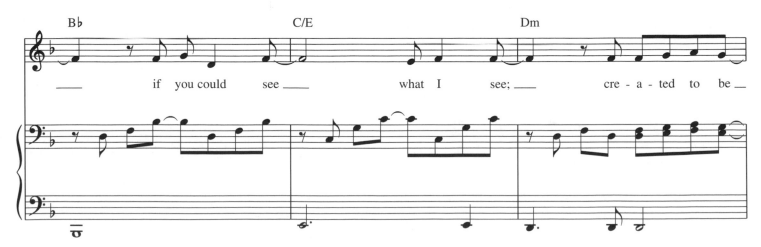

the on - ly one _ for me,

if you could see _ what I see. _

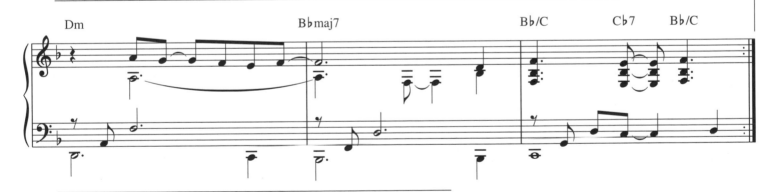

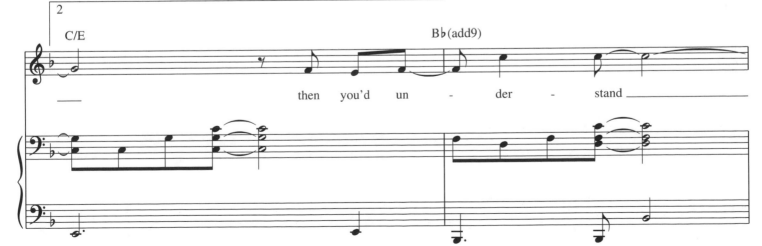

then you'd un - der - stand _

why I fall ____ down to ____ my knees; ____

_____ and I pray __ my love __ will be wor - thy of ____ the

One who gave _____ His life _____ so our love _____ could be. ____

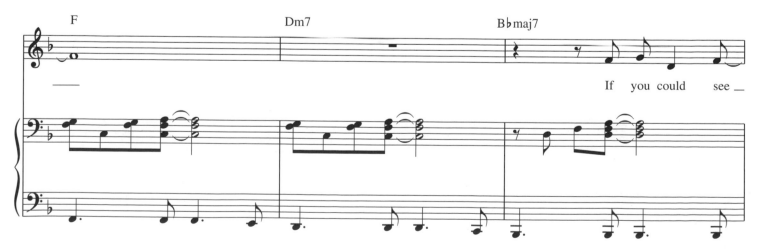

____ If you could see __

see.

If beau-ty is all _____ in the eye _ of _____ the be-hold - er, then I _____ am be-hold - ing true beau - ty. _____

My Place Is With You

Recorded by Clay Crosse

Words and Music by Michael Puryear
and Geoffrey Thurman

'Cause ev - 'ry____ path I've tak - en,_____
What - ev - er lies____ I've lived for,_____

they all____ have led me_____ to_____ know - ing
I have fi - n'lly found the_____ truth: I_____ know____

my_____ place,_ my place_ is with you.____
my_____ place,_ my place_ is with you.

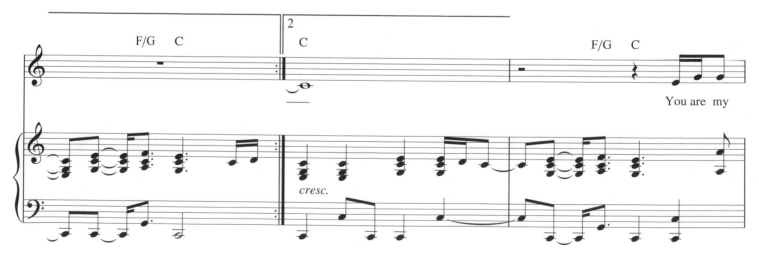

You are my

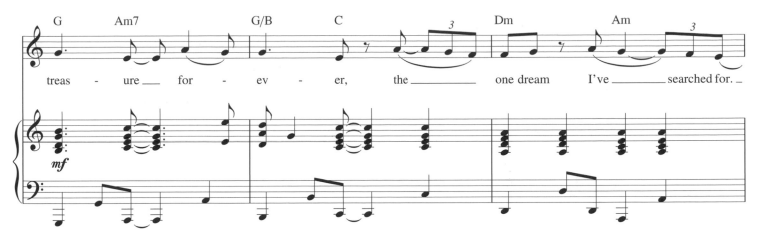

treas - ure ___ for - ev - er, the _____ one dream I've _____ searched for. _

I've not been giv - en my _____ to - mor - rows, _____

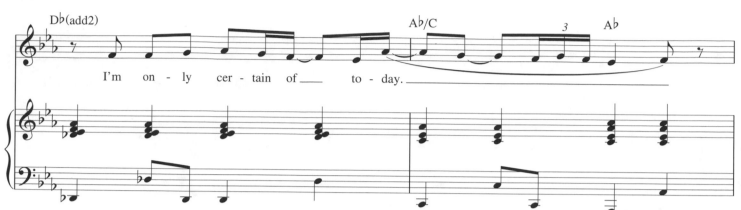

I'm on-ly cer-tain of ____ to - day. ____

And if I don't see an -oth - er sun - rise, ____

I will not have to be _____ a - fraid. _____

I _____ know __ we will be _____ to - geth - er _____

when all ___ my days ___ are through. _____ I _____ know _

my _____ place, _____ my place_ is with you. ___

My place_ is with you. _____ My place_ is with you. ___

My place ___ is with you.

Love of My Life

Recorded by Michael W. Smith

Words and Music by Jim Brickman
and Tom Douglas

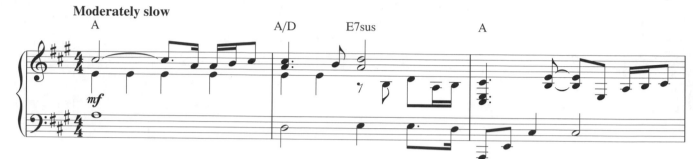

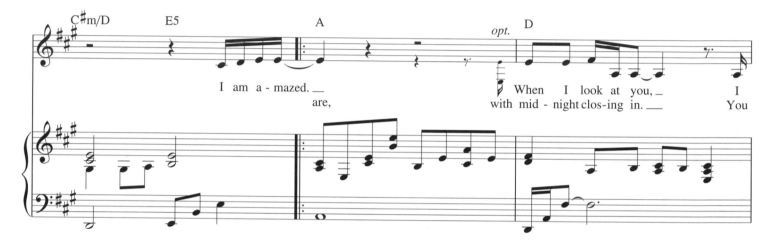

I am a-mazed. ___
are,
with mid-night clos-ing in. ___ When I look at you, ___ I
You

see you smil-ing back at me. It's like all my dreams ___ come true. ___ I am a-fraid
take my hand as our shad-ows dance, with moon-light on ___ your skin. ___ I look in your eyes. ___

I'm if I lost you girl, ___ I'd
lost in-side your kiss. ___ I

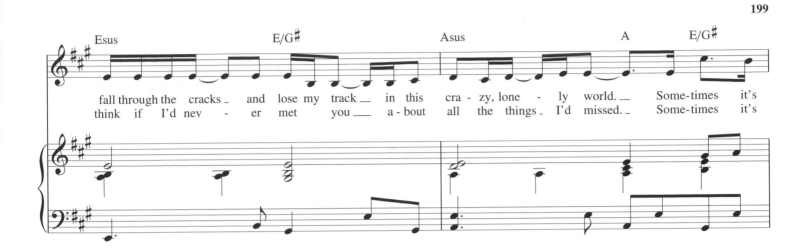

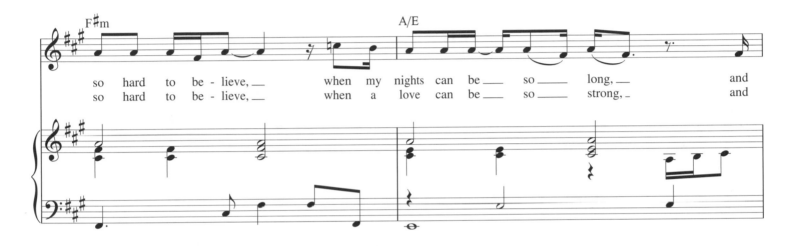

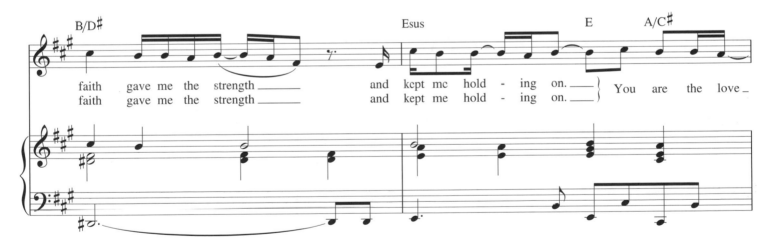

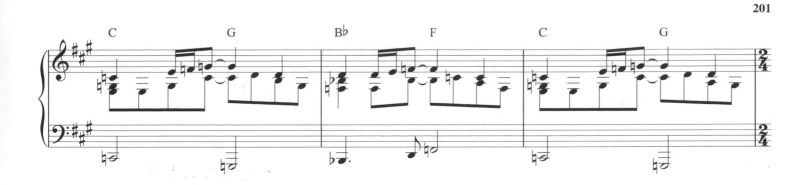

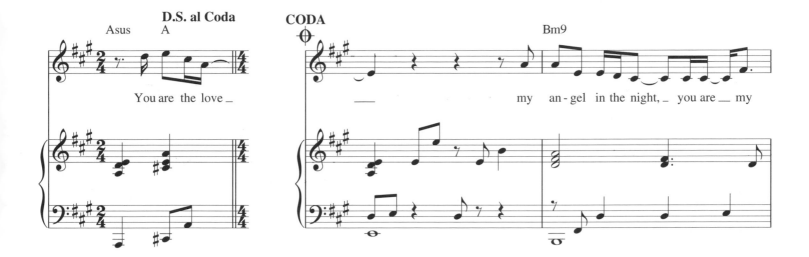

D.S. al Coda

CODA

You are the love __

__ my an-gel in the night, __ you are __ my

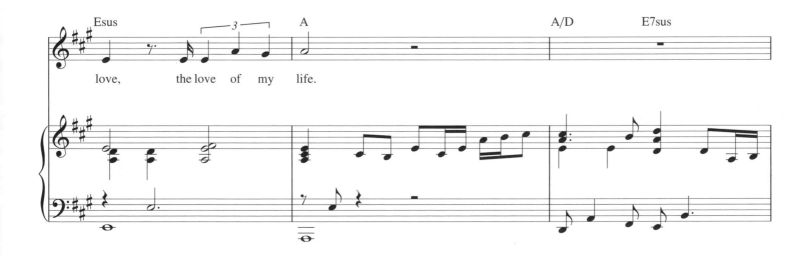

love, the love of my life.

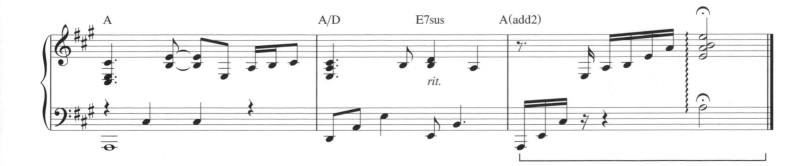

Parent's Prayer
(Let Go of Two)
Recorded by Steven Curtis Chapman

Words and Music by
Greg Davis

I guess we have al - ways known _ that a day like this _ one would come, _
Now in your ten - der care, _ Lord, _ be all that we _ can - not be. _

when our chil - dren would leave _ us and be -
And help us to trust _ You when we don't

gin to build a home of their own. _ Lord, all _ You have taught
see You quick - ly meet - ing their needs. _ For You _ have pro - vid -

us ___ we have glad - ly passed ___ on to them. ___
ed ___ since the day You gave our chil - dren to us. ___

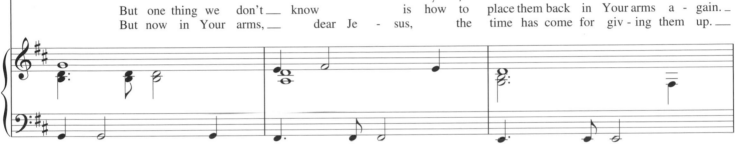

But one thing we don't ___ know is how to place them back in Your arms a - gain. ___
But now in Your arms, ___ dear Je - sus, the time has come for giv - ing them up. ___

Lord, help us let go of two ___ that they might ___ be - come one,

just like the Fa - ther, Spir - it and Son. ___ Two hearts in - vis - i - bly bound ___

be - come   one,   just like the Fa - ther, Spir - it and Son. __
be - come   one,) __

Two hearts in - vis - i - bly bound __ in love by a vow that will not be un - done, __

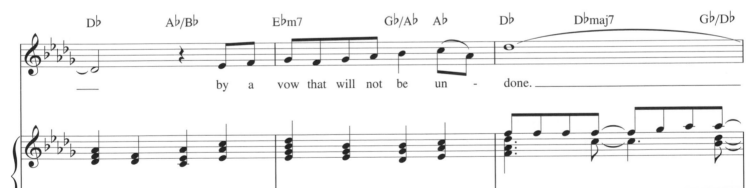

__   by a vow that will not be un - done. __

rit.

This Day

Recorded by Jadon Lavik

Words and Music by
Jadon Lavik

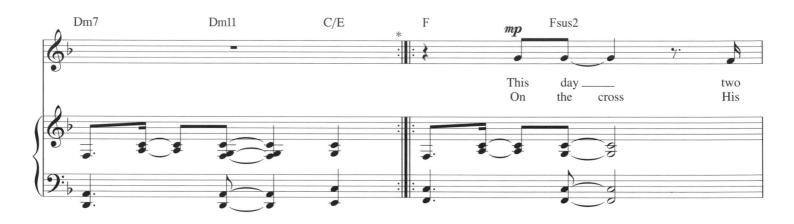

This day _____ two
On the cross _____ His

lives be-come _____ one. _____   This day _____ a new
love was _____ shown. _____   This love _____ will _____

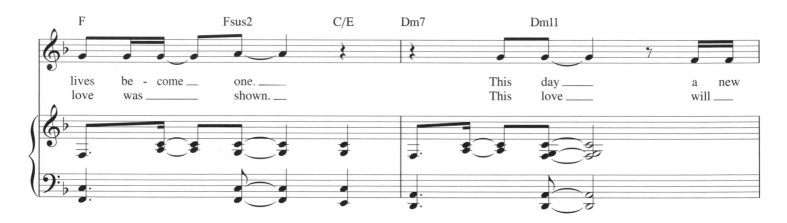

jour-ney has _____ be-gun. _____   Our hearts, _____ full of
build _____ our _____ home. _____   Stand-ing now _____ in

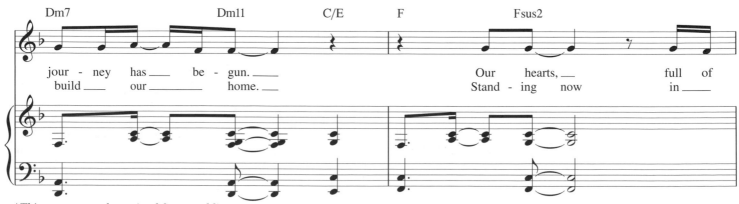

This repeat may be omitted for a wedding.

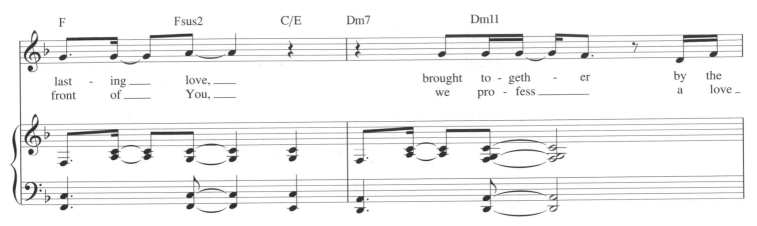

last - ing ___ love, ___
front of ___ You, ___
brought to - geth - er by the
we pro - fess ___ a love ___

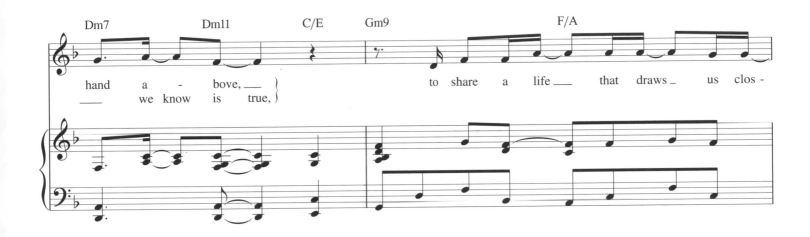

hand a - bove, ___ }
___ we know is true, }
to share a life ___ that draws ___ us clos -

- er ___
to the One ___ that we ___ live ___

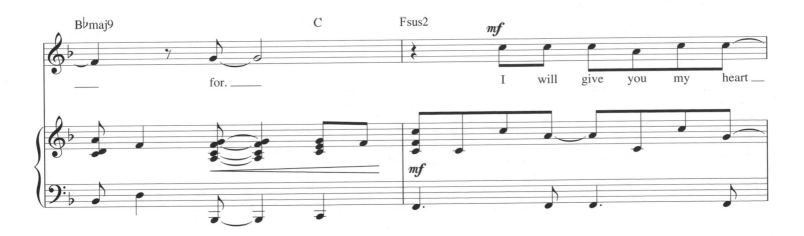

for. ___
I will give you my heart ___

and all of who __ I am. __ I will give more than vows __

and words could ev - er say. __ Yes, I give __ you __ my all __

on this day. __

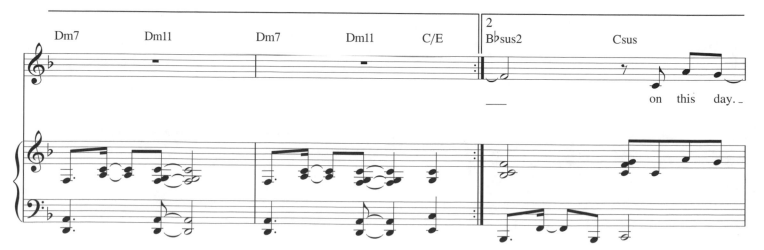

on this day. __

And I give you my all ___ on this ___ day. ___

I will give you my heart ___ and all of who I am. ___

I will give more than vows ___ and words could ev - er say. ___

___ Yes, I give ___ you ___ my all ___ I will give you my heart ___

___ and all of who ___ I am. ___ I will give more than vows ___

___ and words could ev - er say. ___ Yes, I give ___ you ___ my all ___

on this day. _____ And I'll give _____ you _____ my all _____

on this day. _____

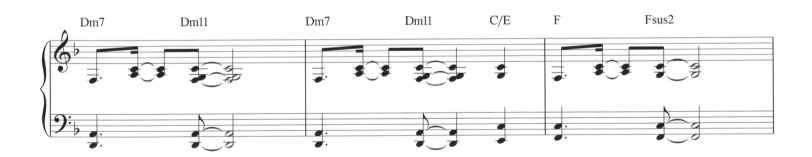

This Is the Day
(A Wedding Song)
Recorded by Scott Wesley Brown

Words and Music by
Scott Wesley Brown

Moderately fast, flowing

This is the day __ that the Lord __ hath __ made, __ and
This is the love __ that the Lord __ hath __ made; __ and that

I'm so __ glad __ He made you. _____ With
you and __ I, _____ we are one. _____

each ris- in' sun you are here by my side, you are
Love's mys- ter- y is un- fold- ing to- day,

more than a dream _ come _ true.
writ - ten for us _ in the Son.

Oh, _____ to
Oh, _____ for

have you, to hold _ you, _ to love you, to pray, _
bet - ter, for worse, _____ for rich or for poor; _

to

share with, to care _ with, to hold hands _ and say: _____
each day that pass - es I'll love _ you more, _____

'cause

this is the day _____ that the Lord hath _ made,

and

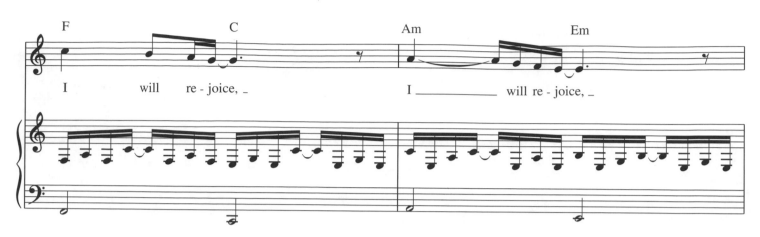

I will re-joice, ___ I ___ will re-joice, ___

I ___ will re-joice ___ with you.

you. This is the day, ___

this is the day, ___

this is the day, _

this is the day. _